AN ANVIL ORIGINAL

Under the general editorship of Louis L. Snyder

EARLY
CHRISTIANITY

ROLAND H. BAINTON †
Titus Street Professor of Ecclesiastical History
Yale University

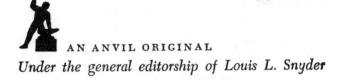

KRIEGER PUBLISHING COMPANY
MALABAR, FLORIDA

Original Edition 1960
Reprint Edition 1984

Printed and Published by
ROBERT E. KRIEGER PUBLISHING COMPANY, INC.
KRIEGER DRIVE
MALABAR, FLORIDA 32950

Copyright © 1960 by Roland H. Bainton
Reprinted by arrangement with Wadsworth Inc.

Printed in the United States of America

Library of Congress Cataloging in Publication Data

Bainton, Roland Herbert, 1894 -
    Early Christianity.

    "An Anvil original."
    Reprint. Originally published: New York: Van Nostrand, c1960.
    Bibliography: p.
    Includes index.
    1. Church history—Primitive and early church, ca. 30-600.
2. Church history—Primitive and early church, ca. 30-600—Sources.
I. Title.
BR165.B275   1984   270.1   83-25150
ISBN 0-89874-735-X

10   9   8   7

TABLE OF CONTENTS

PART I—EARLY CHRISTIANITY

PART II—DOCUMENTS AND READINGS

.

Part I
EARLY CHRISTIANITY

INTRODUCTION

The Rise of Christianity. The Roman historian Tacitus, writing early in the second century of our era, gives an account of the rise of Christianity. It occurs in connection with the relation of the great fire in Rome under Nero, who to allay suspicion that he had started it himself, threw the blame upon a people called Christians. Tacitus reports that the name was taken from Christ who had been executed in Judaea in the reign of Tiberius by the decree of the Procurator Pontius Pilate. Far from being suppressed this noxious superstition flowed along with the scum of the empire to Rome. (*See Document No. 1, I.*)

From this passage we learn that Tacitus considered Christianity to be a religion. He calls it a "noxious superstition." It was a new religion. He locates its rise in Palestine but does not connect it with Judaism. In point of time it began in the reign of Tiberius (A.D. 14-37) during the procuratorship of Pontius Pilate (A.D. 26-36). Other sources enable us to be more precise because by universal testimony the crucifixion occurred on a Passover Friday. This fixes the year with the reasonable certainty at A.D. 30, though we cannot be absolutely sure because the Jews periodically adjusted the lunar and the solar year by the intercalation of an extra month. From Tacitus we learn further that the new religion was extensive and in a quarter of a century had spread from Palestine to Rome.

To locate the rise of a religion in Judaea is at once to connect it with Judaism and as a matter of fact the Church is the daughter of the synagogue. Jesus was a pious Jew who like his people went up to Jerusalem for the great religious festivals. The cardinal affirmations of Judaism became those of Christianity. The first and the greatest was an absolute monotheism. "Hear O Israel, the Lord our God is one Lord" (Deut. 6:4). He is a jealous

9

God who brooks no rivals. The Israelite who seduced his
people to worship the gods of the heathen should be
stoned (Deut. 13). Undeviating devotion to the one God
has been at once the glory and the tragedy of the Jews.
A like intransigence explained the persecution and the
triumph of the early Christians.

This God is a transcendent God, high and lifted up
above the circle of the earth. Before him the nations are
as grasshoppers. God is not to be identified with everything that is. Some aspects of life He blesses and some
He consumes in his anger. God is personal; He is a God
who speaks, who delivered the law to Moses, who carried
on dialogues with Abraham or Jacob. He is the creator
who made the world and saw it to be good. Judaism is
thus an affirmative religion with reference to the world
and life within it. There are religions for which the world
is a prison and the body a tomb. The corresponding ethic
is ascetic. In Judaism there is no trace of asceticism, for
when God had finished the creation he saw everything
that he had made and, "Behold, it was very good" (Gen.
1:31). Yet it did not so continue, for Adam and Eve fell
away from God's commands and thereafter were compelled to live under restrictions. The world then is good
but may be abused. The ethic of Judaism is, therefore,
one not of renunciation but of disciplined employment of
that which God has made.

Judaism is a religion of history which sees the primary
disclosures of God in events. There are religions that seek
God in nature, and others that reach after him by way
of contemplation. The religions of nature discern the
Divine in the movements of the heavenly bodies and in
the rhythm of the seasons. The devotees of these religions
seek to identify themselves with the god of nature by the
adoration of the sun and the stars or by participation in
the recurrent phenomena of springtime fertility. Hence
these religions frequently have rites of sexual licence.
Such was the cult of the Baalim in Palestine. Wherefore
in the name of the God who is above the seasons Elijah
slew the priests of Baal. On the other hand are the
religions of contemplation which seek God from within.
The physical world for them is not a mirror but a veil.
By abstraction from all that is of the senses they strive

to enter into the ineffable. Of such mysticism there is not a trace in the Old Testament.

Rather in its pages God is the God who has made Himself known throughout the course of history. The great religious festivals of Judaism are memorials of the deeds of God. Passover commemorates the deliverance from Egypt when the Lord God with a mighty hand and an outstretched arm released his people from bondage, led them dry-shod through the Red Sea waters, through the wilderness into the land of promise. Some of the Psalms are simply recitals of the mighty acts of God. These deeds were done on behalf of Israel. The interventions and self disclosures of God were not uniform and universal. Not at all times nor in all places had He made Himself known, but with Israel He had made a covenant that they should be to Him "a peculiar people, a Holy people unto the Lord thy God" (Deut. 26:18-19). Judaism in the time of the prophets was universalized and Amos declared that as God had brought Israel up from Egypt, so He had brought the Philistines from Capthor and the Syrians from Kir (Amos 9:7). Yet it was not by the recognition of the validity of all religions that Judaism was universalized, but rather by the invitation to all peoples to accept the yoke of the law and to make their pilgrimage to Mount Zion.

Increasingly the law became the focus of Judaism because captivity cut off access to Jerusalem. Whereas the Temple could not be moved but only replaced by the synagogue, the law could be elaborated and practiced as well in Babylon as in Jerusalem, the Holy City. The marvel of the Jewish people is that they survived even to the time of Christ, for during the previous seven centuries they had lacked political autonomy and had been subject to deportation. Where now are the Amalekites, the Moabites, or the Philistines? The Jews, and from all the ancient cultures of the Near East the Jews alone, survive to this day. And it has been because of their tenacious loyalty to the worship of the one God and their observance of His law, which the more detailed it became the more it served to set them off as a peculiar people.

The greatest seduction for the Jews, as for all minorities, is not the hostility but the friendliness of neighbors.

The Philistines would honor Yahweh if the Jews would reciprocate as to Melkart. The intermarriage of royal families carried with it an interchange of gods. Political isolationism was necessary, therefore, in order to preserve religious purity. But such aloofness is difficult to maintain in a world where existence appears to depend on political alliances. All the other communities of the Near East fraternized, appropriated each others gods, and perished. The Jews held to a line of rigidity but only at the cost of civil war. Alexander the Great had envisaged a cultural mingling of the people of the Near East. The Greeks, the Persians, the Jews, the Egyptians should be mixed in a common bowl. None need renounce his own heritage but should add to it that of the others. Some Jews were willing. They were of no mind to repudiate Yahweh. They would simply add Melkart. But to worship any other god in addition to Yahweh was apostasy punishable by death. Therefore the father of the Maccabees slew a fellow Jew and started the great rebellion which for a brief period restored the political independence of Israel only later to be lost again to the Romans. The melting pot assimilation of Judaism to Hellenic culture had been rejected.

But there was another way of Hellenization, namely in the realm of ideas and we find it in Philo of Alexandria, a contemporary of St. Paul. Philo was a loyal Jew who kept the law and the feasts, but he combined Judaism with Hellenic philosophy by the devise of allegory, thereby converting the Old Testament narratives into Platonic myths. Far from supposing that he was borrowing from the Greeks, Philo assumed that the Greeks had borrowed from the Jews and that Plato had taken his ideas from Moses. Historically, of course, this view is quite untenable, but the significance of Philo cannot be overemphasized because he was the first to combine the Hebraic and the Hellenic strands which run through the whole fabric of Western thought and have constituted a perpetual tension within Christianity itself.

The philosophy of the ancient world from which Philo drew was itself varied and by his time the many systems had come to be blended. For later Christian thought three strains are highly important. From Plato comes the view of the realm of ideas set off from the world of the phenomenal which is but an imperfect copy of the archetype. This distinction corresponds to that between the material and the immaterial. In the Platonic tradition the note is persistent that the body is a clog. Immortality is the separation of the soul from the body. But if ultimate reality is the archetypal idea how is the transition effected from the noumenal to the phenomenal? The answer was, by way of intermediaries. This concept in late Judaism fastened upon Wisdom as God's agent. She was almost personalized, for the impersonal was not congenial to Hebrew thought. In the book of the Wisdom of Solomon she is God's agent in the creation and it is she who, "in all ages enters into Holy souls and makes them friends of God and prophets." Stoicism, though pantheistic had a concept which could be associated with Wisdom. It was the principle of rationality which pervades the cosmos and in man enables him to comprehend the world and direct his own affairs. The word for this principle was *logos* which means both reason and word. Since this reason is implanted in all men they are capable of recognizing and practicing a universal morality, called the law of nature. The third system of importance was that of Aristotle who profoundly affected the high Middle Ages but enjoyed less influence in the early Christian period.

Although Judaism in Alexandria appropriated many of these strands the Judaism of Palestine increasingly rejected the wisdom of the world and looked for vindication at the hands of God. The Jews had always held that God's mighty deeds were not restricted to the past. They looked forward to the great day of the Lord when their enemies would be trodden under foot. Their hopes centered upon a redeemer. He might be a king of the line of David. He might be meek and lowly, riding upon an ass. He might be a sacrificial figure who should make expiation for his people that by his stripes they might be healed, and again He might be a semi-divine figure called indeed a Son of Man but coming on the clouds of heaven. Such hopes were especially congenial to the Qumran community lately disclosed in the Dead Sea Scrolls.

But when would the deliverer come? How should the day of the Lord be brought about? Could man hasten its coming? A world revolution would be required to bring it to pass because Palestine was an occupied country under the arms of Rome. If Palestine were to be free Rome would have to be expelled from the Near East. Some of the Jews, namely the Sadducees, expected help neither from men nor from God but thought the best course was to fraternize with the Romans. Others thought that the Lord would intervene to crown with victory an insurrection as once he had done for the Maccabees. These were the Zealots. Still others thought that Israel should neither fraternize nor rebel, but should keep the law and wait for vindication at the hands of God. This was the party of the Pharisees.

At the time when Christ was born feeling ran high. The flower of Jewish youth had been destroyed in the previous century during the Roman civil wars, which lead to the establishment of the empire. Jewish rebellions against Rome had been crushed by wholesale crucifixions. Then a decree went out from Augustus Caesar that all the world should be enrolled. This census was designed to assess the military potential and to levy taxes. At that very time Christ was born.

The records of his life are preserved for us in the Four Gospels, Matthew, Mark, Luke, and John. Their literary relations are highly intricate and baffling. The common view, though sometimes challenged, is that Mark was a source for Matthew and for Luke and that in addition they had another source called Q from which is derived that which they have in common and perhaps also that which is peculiar to each. John's Gospel stands apart as rather an interpretation and a narrative. This total body of material is not adequate for a detailed biography but the main outline emerges with clarity. None of this material nor indeed any of the New Testament is included in the documents in this booklet because if there is any source of early Christianity which should be read without abridgment, it is the New Testament and it is universally available.

From the Gospels we learn that Jesus was a Jewish teacher who sided politically with the Pharisees against fraternization with Rome and against rebellion. He differed from the Pharisees as to what was entailed in the keeping of the law, whose meticulous enactments served neither God nor man. "The Sabbath was made for man, not man for the Sabbath." At the same time the ethical demands of Judaism were intensified beyond the level of human attainment. In the realm of act there must be readiness to sell all and give to the poor, to resist not evil, and renounce retaliation. In the realm of thought there must be purity and selflessness. One should refrain not only from adultery and murder but from lust and hate.

The fulfillment of these demands was not regarded as a way of forcing God's hand as if He would intervene only after men had shown themselves thus fully obedient. The point was rather that the disciples should be ready when the Lord did come. "Repent; the Kingdom of God is at hand." In some sense God's Kingdom was regarded as already present. Yet, it was to be dramatically manifested in spectacular fashion within the lifetime of that very generation when the Son of Man should appear.

Did Jesus identify Himself with this figure? Some of His references to the Son of Man do not require that He was speaking of Himself—others do. Were these latter introduced into the narrative by the evangelists who wrote after the Christians had all come to be persuaded that their Master was the Son of Man? What role did Jesus envisage for Himself? He protested against being placed upon a par with God, "Why callest thou Me good? None is good but God." Yet He rejoiced in the confession of Peter that He was the Christ, that is the Messiah, the expected deliverer. How then was He to deliver His people?

We know only that He set His face to go up to Jerusalem. That there He drove the money-changers from the temple. He did not then proceed to challenge the Romans by organizing an insurrection. He simply sat in the temple and taught, witnessing to God's truth. That was His role. All else was committed to the hands of God. The opposition quickly consolidated. The high priests could not tolerate His interference with racketeering in the temple courts. The Zealots could not forgive a leader who would only teach and not fight. The Pharisees considered Him an apostate because in their eyes He broke the law. But none of these considerations would condemn

Him with the Romans who alone had the power to inflict His execution. They would act only if He were a political menace. The charge must therefore center on His Messianic pretensions and He who said, "resist not evil" was crucified through the fear that He was the focus of a rebellion.

In the crisis His disciples failed. Judas betrayed Him. Peter denied, and the others fled. Yet to Peter first appeared the risen Lord. The accounts of the resurrection are of three kinds. Two center on localities and the question is whether the first appearances were in Galilee or in Jerusalem. Curiously, the earliest manuscripts of the Gospel of Mark have no account of the resurrection but conclude with the verse, "Neither said they [the women at the tomb] anything to any man for they were afraid." The women had not seen the risen Lord but had learned from an angel that He would appear in Galilee. Presumably the ensuing account related such an appearance, but it has been supplanted in the present Gospel by the tradition which later became dominant of the first appearance at the tomb near Jerusalem. The third type is the experience of the Apostle Paul who counted himself a witness of the resurrection but gives no details of sight or sound, testifying merely that the Lord had appeared unto him.

The resurrection made the Church. Perhaps without it there might have been a church, for Paul tells us that the Lord appeared to 500 brethren at once. They had assembled before their experience of the resurrection. The cross had brought them together, but would they have remained together, would they have established a new religion had they proclaimed only Christ crucified and not also Christ risen from the dead?

The beginning of the Church is dated, however, not directly from the experience of the resurrection but rather from the day of Pentecost when the Spirit as in tongues of flame descended upon the assembled disciples. The risen Christ did not long remain in the same immediacy of contact with His followers as during the first months. His place was taken by the Spirit and to be a Christian meant to be filled with the Spirit. All the offices in the Christian community were gifts of the Spirit.

A church had come into being. It was derived from an act of God. Here was the Jewish conception of God as a doer of mighty deeds. He had become incarnate in Christ and had raised Him from the dead. Who then was this Christ and what was His relation to God? The Messiah, the Son of Man—these were the earliest answers. Paul went further and said that this Christ, having been on an equality with God, emptied Himself taking the form of a servant—here we have again the Jewish picture of the suffering servant—and humbled himself even to the death on the cross. Wherefore God would highly exalt Him (Phil. 2). Yet in the end, God would be all in all. The Son was thus considered as ultimately subordinate to the Father. There is in Paul no mention of the virgin birth nor in the Gospel of Mark which begins with an account of the baptism. The virgin birth is related only in the prologues to the Gospels of Matthew and of Luke. Also in them Jesus is identified functionally with the Wisdom of God so that what, "the Wisdom of God saith," can become a word of Jesus. In the prologue of John's Gospel, Jesus fulfills the role of Wisdom as God's agent in the creation and of entering into the souls of men but the word there used is not Wisdom but *logos,* the immanent reason of the Stoics. More however is affirmed than ever was said of Wisdom or of the *logos.* For the Word became flesh. Here there is no despising of the flesh as a tomb. John's Gospel thus proclaimed the doctrine of the incarnation.

A New Religion. The Church had come into being. But did it constitute a new religion? Or was it rather the true Judaism? All the central affirmations of Judaism reappeared in Christian teaching. That God is one, God is exalted; God speaks; God created the world and found it good; man fell and must subject himself in the use of the world to disciplined restraint; God acts in history. The greatest act of God was the fulfillment of the Messianic hope of Israel in Jesus Christ. At this point began the divergence of Christianity from Judaism whose leaders would not concede that an enthusiast crucified at the instigation of the Sanhedrin was the promised Messiah. The resurrection of Jesus was also denied, though as such it was not so offensive as the Messianic claim, because Elisha in the Old Testament had raised the widow's son.

The Jewish hope for the last times was not basically altered because the view was retained that the new age would transform the whole structure of society and was yet to come. But the form was different in that the Messiah had already appeared and the eschatological hope had reference·to His return. The greatest historical event to be commemorated was no longer the deliverance of Israel from Egypt but the redemption of mankind by Christ. For that reason the Passover was superseded by Easter. And since the Lord appeared of the first day of the week, this rather than the seventh day became the Sabbath.

As for the Jewish law, with all of its dietary regulations, there was much debate in Christian circles. Jesus had observed the law except in extreme situations where it conflicted with the obligation of man to man. The Apostle Paul went further and contended that through Christ the law was at an end, because man cannot be saved by the keeping of the commands of the law but only through faith in Christ. The law served an historical purpose by setting up a moral standard which confronted man with the ideal, convicted him of failure, induced repentance and humility and thus prepared the way for faith. The Jews might indeed continue to observe the law if they so desired, but it should not be made binding upon the Gentiles to whom also the gospel must be proclaimed. Judaism likewise sought proselytes among the Gentiles, but enjoined upon them the keeping of the law. Paul insisted at this point on "the liberty with which Christ hath made us free" (Gal. 5:1). Peter agreed that the law did not apply to the Gentile converts, but in Paul's eyes Peter was inconsistent in holding that the Jewish Christian should continue to observe it and that when Jews and Gentiles were together, the Gentiles should conform. Paul won and among Christians the Jewish law fell into abeyance. From the Jewish point of view this was very serious because the law was the symbol and the focus of Jewish singularity in the worship of the one true God.

Hence the Sanhedrin disowned the Nazarenes, that is the followers of Jesus of Nazareth. The designation "Christian" first arose in Gentile Antioch. Persecution began. Stephen, the first Christian martyr, was stoned in Jerusalem by the Jews in accord with the command of Deuteronomy 13 that any Israelite, who enticed his people to go after the gods of the heathen, should be "stoned with stones that he die." Paul stood consenting to Stephen's death and then set out for Damascus seeking other victims. On the way, that Jesus whom he persecuted, laid hold upon him and the great persecutor began to be the great apostle. The death of Stephen scattered the disciples and marked the beginning of the great missionary enterprise in which Paul took the Gentile world as his province. He had been born in Tarsus outside of Palestine and was by birth a citizen of Rome. He was bilingual, but Greek is the language of all of his letters. This of itself marked no departure from Judaism because the Jews had long since been dispersed throughout the empire and Greek was the language of the Hellenistic Jews particularly at Alexandria. The Greek translation of the Old Testament, called the Septuagint, because supposedly executed by a committee of seventy men, was their Bible. It was Paul's Bible and it became the Bible of the Christian Church. Paul always made his approach first through the synagogues. When rejected there, as he invariably was, he turned to the Gentiles. Thus, Christianity passed from Palestine to the Greco-Roman world and in the congregations the proportion of Gentiles increased.

— 1 —

THE CHURCH IN THE AGE OF PERSECUTION

The Roman Government and the Christians in the First and Second Centuries. Was Christianity to be regarded in the Roman Empire as a new religion? The Jews insisted that it was not Judaism. Christians were equally emphatic that their religion was the true Judaism, that they preached nothing which had not been foretold by Moses and the Prophets. How should the Roman authorities view the case? The matter was brought to their attention by disturbances of the peace. The Jews would riot against the Christians. So also would the pagans because the Christians were more aggressive than the Jews in attacks upon idolatry. Yet in the eyes of the pagans, the Christians were still Jews. The heathen at Thessalonica said, "these men *being Jews* do considerably trouble our city" (Acts 16:20). The Roman governors so regarded them and when the Jews dragged Paul before Gallio, the Roman proconsul in Greece, he dismissed the case as simply a dispute within Judaism (Acts 18:12-17).

The time at which the Romans became aware of the rise of a new religion cannot be fixed with precision. Tacitus in his account already mentioned of the fire at Rome under Nero in the year 64, assumed that the Christians were known to be a distinct group. But Tacitus was writing fifty years after the event and may have read back the knowledge available in his own time. In the absence of contrary evidence we can do no better than to accept his version. By the 60's, then, we may assume that Christianity had emerged as a new religion in the Roman Empire.

Such recognition brought with it a great difference in the treatment accorded the Christians by the Roman government. Until then Rome appeared as the protector of the Christians against the Jews. Thereafter Rome became the great persecutor. The change was derived from the entire religious policy of Rome. The cardinal principle throughout antiquity was that the state can prosper only through the favor of the gods. The warfare of peoples was considered to be a warfare between their gods. A state would be wise, therefore, to make an *entente cordiale* with the powers of heaven. Rome, as she conquered the peoples, had no desire to alienate their gods and might adopt them for herself, as the cult of the Great Mother was introduced from Asia Minor in order that Cybele might avert Hannibal. Certainly all religions were to be tolerated in the lands of their origin, provided their practices did not contravene the laws of Rome as in the case of human sacrifice among the Druids. At the same time Rome and Italy felt an aversion to an inundation by oriental deities especially those whose rites were of an orgiastic nature. The cult of the Great Mother was subjected to restrictions when its Bacchanalian character came to light. Yet it was not suppressed. The policy came to be one of discrimination. Religions which had long since spread throughout the empire were authorized. New religions were unauthorized, even though no law made the express distinction between *religiones licitae et illicitae.* Judaism was one of the recognized religions. Christianity, if it were not Judaism, would be an unrecognized religion and subject therefore to police measures.

The grounds on which the Roman government at first interfered with the new religion are not too clear. The charge that the Christians had burned Rome was specific but could not affect them outside of Rome. And Tacitus adds that the persecution continued, less on the ground of arson than of hatred of the human race, *odium generis humani,* a charge leveled at sorcerers.

By the end of the first century, however, the grounds of persecution become quite specific. Our first clear light on the subject is afforded by a letter of Pliny the Proconsul in Bithynia to the Emperor Trajan around the year 112. (*See Document No. 1, II.*) Pliny's letter makes it plain that the sole offense for which the Christians were put to death was their refusal to worship the emperor. He says that he does not know whether Christians should be punished for the name or for the crimes associated with the name, for example, arson. But he does punish simply for the name and the test is whether the accused refuses to curse Christ and worship the emperor.

The imperial cult had become the focus of the persecution. This cult meant much to Rome as a device for securing religious uniformity throughout the empire. Though each people might be allowed its own indigenous cult, how advantageous it would be for imperial unity if there were at the same time one cult in which all of the peoples could participate! No one of the many religions of the empire had sufficient universality to be adopted for the purpose save the worship of the deified ruler. The concept had its origin in the deification of the founders of the Greek city-states. Alexander the Great combined this practice with the prostration accorded to the emperors of Persia and the deification of the Pharaohs in Egypt. Julius Caesar, who greatly admired Alexander, saw in these concepts a device for legitimatizing power and identified himself with Jupiter. He found it easier to become a god than to become a king. Augustus laid hold of the idea with certain concessions to old Roman feeling. The emperor was deemed to become fully a god only after his death, while on earth he was attended by a divine spirit. That was why Vespasian when asked on his death bed how he felt replied "I feel as if I am about to become a god." Local Roman patriotism was curried by the identification of Augustus with Romulus, the divine founder of Rome. With these modifications the cult was imposed upon the empire. It met with no opposition in the west and was greeted with enthusiasm in the east by all save the Jews. When Pilate sought to introduce into the temple enclosure standards bearing the insignia of the divine ruler, the Jewish leaders prostrated themselves before him saying that he would first have to remove their heads. Pilate yielded. Caligula, in A.D. 41, announced that he would erect his statue in the temple at Jerusalem to be worshiped. The Jews were on the point of revolt when Caligula was assassinated. Thereafter, by tacit consent, the Jews became exempt from the requirements of the imperial cult. The monotheism of Judaism had conquered in its refusal to deify the ruler.

If Christianity were Judaism it might enjoy a like exemption but if it were a new religion then death was the penalty for refusal to comply. The conflict became sharper than in the case of Judaism for the Christians added to the Jewish formulation "Hear, O Israel, the Lord thy God is one Lord" the further confession, "Christ is Lord." Not only the God of heaven and earth but a malefactor crucified by the government of Rome was declared to have an authority exceeding that of the emperor of Rome. The cult of Christ and the cult of Caesar were incompatible. In practice the Christian refusal might appear to have been no more intolerable to Rome than the Jewish. But there were special reasons for dealing tenderly with the Jews. During the first century they were still a nation and a very truculent nation. In that day the Jews were not charged with avarice but with turbulence. Yet their insurgence did not seriously menace the empire. Titus took Jerusalem in A.D. 70, and after the revolt of Bar Kochba, early in the second century, Jerusalem was razed and the Jews ceased to be a nation in the political sense. In the dispersion they gained a few proselytes but not an alarming number, whereas Christianity was gaining among the Gentiles. If it continued to spread it might subvert the majority of the populace. And, in that case, if Christians continued to reject the imperial cult the government would be confronted with one of three alternatives; to exterminate the Christians, to abandon the imperial cult and secularize the state, or to make Christianity itself the state religion.

These alternatives had not clearly emerged by the time of Pliny. The menace appeared to him to be manageable. He found in the Christians an inflexible obstinacy in adherence to a depraved superstition. He noticed that some persons in the area had given up Christianity twenty years previously. The measures which he had taken were proving instrumental in a pagan revival. The emperor agreed with him. The nonconformity of the Christians could not be tolerated if it came to public attention, but the matter was not sufficiently serious to warrant a search for subversives.

The policy announced by the Emperor Trajan continued to govern the policy of Rome throughout the second century. Persecution was not systematic but sporadic and was directed more against the leaders of the Church than against the congregations. One is amazed, for example, by the treatment of Ignatius, Bishop of Antioch in Syria, who was brought across Asia Minor and Thrace to be devoured by beasts at Rome. On the way be was allowed to visit the churches and to communicate with Bishop Polycarp of Smyrna, who himself did not suffer until some forty years later. Yet, if the hostility of the Jews and the pagans stirred up the populace, the government would take action, including not only execution but torture.

Several reliable accounts are extant of the sufferings of the Christians during the second century. One may wonder that such details are available. The account of the execution of Polycarp was written by his own congregation immediately after the event and one observes that it was only the shepherd and not the flock that was immolated. The story of the outbursts at Lyons and Vienne came also from survivors. The report of the trial of Justin is the more amazing because here we have a dialogue between the judge and the accused. Such a stenographic report might well have been transcribed by a Christian in the court room who would not have been molested unless he had been specifically accused. Or again the public stenographer might have been sufficiently well disposed to allow the making of a copy. Often enough magistrates were sympathetic to the Christians and reluctantly inflicted only that which the law required.

In the case of Polycarp (*see Document No. 2, I*) observe that at first he withdrew to his country estate. Much debate later arose as to whether Christians might legitimately hide to escape persecution. The magistrate who took Polycarp back to Smyrna had a Christian aunt, Alce. He tried to persuade Polycarp to save himself by saying "Caesar is Lord" and could not understand why the obstinate Christian should make an issue of so trivial a point. When the martyr stood in the arena the proconsul followed the practice outlined in Pliny's letter of giving the accused three opportunities to recant. In the magistrate's eyes the only punishable offense was the refusal to curse Christ and worship the emperor, but the mob raised the cry of atheism on the assumption that those who denied the pagan gods worshiped no gods at all. Not only the heathen but also the Jews were active in trying to prevent the Christians from securing the body of the martyr.

The examination of Justin Martyr (*see Document No. 2, II*) and his companions makes no reference to any mob action. In this instance an intellectual was tried by an intellectual. Justin was one of the great early Christian theologians. Rusticus, the judge, was a philosopher and friend of the Emperor Marcus Aurelius. But the debate did not center on theology. Rusticus asked what the Christians believed, but when Justin started upon an exposition the Prefect cut him off abruptly with the question "Where do you meet?" The fact that Justin was a Christian was of itself sufficient to secure his condemnation. The only further point of interest was to elicit information about other members of the congregation. One notes their adroit evasiveness in testifying as to others. But there was nothing evasive about their own affirmations of faith. How incredible to a Roman magistrate must have been the absurd truculence of those who contemned his jurisdiction and reminded him that he would someday have to stand before "the more terrible judgment seat of our Lord and Savior who shall judge the whole world."

The persecution at Lyons and Vienne in Gaul (not Vienna in Austria) was prompted by mob action. (*See Document No. 2, III.*) A new charge was introduced that the Christians were guilty of "Thyestean banquets and Oedipodean intercourse." The first signifies the eating of babies and the charge arose because the Christians at the sacrament of the Lord's Supper "ate flesh and drank blood." The second accusation had reference to incest, a charge frequently brought against religious groups meeting in secret, as did the Christians who admitted none save the baptized to the Lord's Supper. Because of these charges those who confessed at Lyons and Vienne that they were Christians suffered as Christians but those who denied suffered nevertheless as criminals. One observes in this persecution that no distinction was made for age and sex. Ponticus and Blandina were in their teens. Note that the severity of the government and the intrepidity of the martyrs made converts.

But persecution did not destroy the Christians. The aged bishop Pothinus was executed at Lyons. His place was taken by the great theologian Irenaeus, who fortunately during the outburst had been absent at Rome. The spread of Christianity was such that Tertullian, writing at the turn from the second to the third century could say "The blood of the martyrs is the seed of the church."

Rome and the Christians in the Third Century. The government was compelled, therefore, to adopt a more systematic policy. Whereas during the second century the procedure was one of sporadic police action, the third century saw the emergence of three policies pursued with greater or less consistency. The first may be called that of oriental syncretism. It aimed to revive on the religious level that mingling of cultures which had been the goal of Alexander. As the Seleucids had sought to make Judaism a religion among the religions, so the Severi desired to make Christianity a cult among the cults of the empire. They were ready enough to incorporate Christianity into their pantheon if only Christianity would not be so intolerant with reference to the other religions.

The founder of the dynasty was Septimius Severus (A.D. 193-211). He was married to the daughter of a priest of the Syrian cult. One of the Severi adopted a Semitic name, El Gabal. Alexander Severus was claimed to have had in his private chapel statues of Orpheus, Abraham, and Christ. The story has been called into question but enshrines the truth that he would gladly have mingled paganism, Judaism, and Christianity. This policy could not succeed. Judaism would admit only one God, and Christianity, in addition, only one Lord. Discovering his failure Septimius Severus resolved then to try to check the spread of these two religions and issued an edict directed only against converts.

Then came a period of almost unbroken peace for the church until A.D. 250, when a new policy was tried by the

Emperor Decius, a policy of extermination associated with a number of rulers who had served on the Danubian frontier where Christianity was very sparsely adopted. They were military men to whom the new religion appeared as an enervating cult. Its strength, incidentally, was in the peaceful interior of the empire, particularly in Asia Minor. These emperors, Decius, and later Diocletian, Galerius, and Maximinus Daza, attributed the weakness of the Roman defense to the neglect of the ancient gods who had assured Rome's earlier victories. The deified emperor was of course still among the gods but in these persecutions the imperial cult was not stressed as the crucial point at issue, but rather sacrifice was demanded to the gods in general.

Under Decius a sacrifice was to be required of everyone in the empire, Christian and pagan alike. All were required to have certificates signed by the local magistrate testifying that in his presence the persons named had offered a sacrifice. Over forty of these certificates have survived in Egypt. The one conserved at Yale University is reproduced in Document No. 1, III. Among those named in the extant *libelli*, as these certificates were called, seventeen are women, thirteen are men, one is Roman, eight Greek, and the rest Egyptian. Curiously, everyone has two names, of which one is either Aurelius or Aurelia. This name was assumed in gratitude for the conferring of universal citizenship by the emperor Aurelius Caracalla.

The persecution of Decius caused the frequent apostasy of the larger part of the congregations and had it been long continued might have disproved the dictum that the blood of the martyrs is the seed of the church. But it was brief, as was also another persecution by Valerian in A.D. 258.

The first Edict of Toleration was issued by Gallienus in A.D. 261. (*See Document No. 1, IV.*) Its object was not to favor Christianity but only to oppose it by a different technique—that of propaganda rather than violence. Gallienus belonged to the emperors imbued with Hellenic culture and preferred that the issue be contested in the field of ideas. For this purpose a considerable body of literature lay already at hand.

The Literary Attack on Christianity and the Replies.
The most extensive attack on Christianity to survive from
this period is that written by the eclectic Platonist, Celsus,
around A.D. 177-180. The work in its entirety is lost but
extensive excerpts are fortunately included in the reply by
the Church Father Origen writing around A.D. 246-248.
(*See Document No. 3, 1.*) The attack of Celsus was pas-
sionate and comprehensive. He impugned the intellectual
character of the Christians whom he called bamboozlers
of women, children, and slaves. He impugned the moral
character of Christians. Since they receive ex-robbers, he
said, they must consist of robbers because no robber can
ever be *ex*. Celsus denied the possibility of moral trans-
formation through conversion. He contemned the Jews
but considered the Christians to be worse because the
Jews at least had a country. The Jewish-Christian picture
of the creation he regarded as untenable, for how could
God have numbered the days before he had created the
sun and the moon? The Old Testament says that God
made the world for man: Why not equally for the animals? The Christian picture of redemption appeared to
Celsus to be incredible. The Christians held that God
came to earth. What for? To learn something about it?
To put the world right? Why did he not create a world
that would not need to be put right? And if it were in
need, why did He not think to come sooner? If God were
to come to earth, why should He choose such a miserable
country as Palestine? As for Jesus, he was the illegitimate
child of Mary and a Roman soldier named Penthera
(this name is simply a corruption of the Greek word for
virgin, *parthenos*). Joseph cast her away. She took the
child to Egypt where he learned magic and upon return-
ing to Palestine associated himself with eleven of the
worst rascals in the country. (Origen remarks in his reply
that Celsus was mistaken; there were twelve.) Jesus told
them that if they got into trouble in one town, they should
run to the next. Jesus was betrayed by one of his disciples
and crucified. The Christians said that he would rise from
the dead, but who ever saw him risen? Only one crazy
woman (the reference is to Mary in the Garden). Why
did not Christ appear to Pilate and the Jews? They could
not have hurt him any more. The Christians claimed

Jesus to have been divine, because he predicted his death, but where are the predictions to be found? In the Gospels. And who wrote the Gospels? The disciples. And when? After the event. But suppose that Jesus did predict that he would be crucified. If a robber should foretell that he would be caught and executed and it came to pass, would that make him a son of God? As for the miracles, other people too can work them. What in any case was miraculous about being clothed with purple and being crowned with thorns and given gall and vinegar to drink? The Christians said that God would judge the world and consume the wicked in fire. What a skillful cook He must be to be able to burn half the world without charring the remainder!

Thus Celsus attacked Christian views of creation, redemption, and ultimate destiny. The venom in his attack was derived from the belief that Christians were enemies of society. They held aloof from the common life. They would not accept political responsibility or military service. If all men were as they the empire would be overrun by lawless barbarians. Either Christians should give up having families and go to the desert or else assume their full responsibilities to the state. In other words, they should either be monks or else magistrates and soldiers.

The Christians were thus confronted with a vast range of accusations. The mobs accused them of atheism, cannibalism, and incest. One observes that these vulgar charges do not appear in Celsus. The government branded them as unpatriotic and illegal. The philosophers called them stupid and irresponsible. Against this barrage the Christians erected their barricades. A considerable body of literature survives called the Apologies. (*See Reading No. 3.*) Some are extensive such as the reply to Celsus by Origen of Alexandria, the Apology of Justin in Asia Minor, the Apology of Tertullian and later Arnobius in northern Africa, of Tatian in Syria, and of Athenagoras in Greece; fragments survive of Aristides and Melito of Sardis. Their refutations can be subsumed under a number of heads.

As for the charge of atheism, "that indeed," said the Christians, "is true, if Socrates was an atheist." The point, of course, is that to deny polytheism is not atheism. But

to couple this rejoinder with the name of Socrates was
particularly telling because Christianity thereby was linked
with the Greek philosophical tradition. The denial was
accompanied by a counterblast against popular paganism
with abundant denunciation and ridicule of the immorality, anthropomorphisms, and inconsistencies of the gods.
If Bacchus was made a god for discovering wine, sniffed
Tertullian, "why not Lucullus for importing the cherry
from Pontus?" The modern reader wonders as to the
relevance of the attack which was freely admitted by the
educated pagan. The answer is that the Christians were
appealing to the masses. Furthermore, the cultivated
pagans, though they allegorized the gods, did not abandon
the popular rites.

As for illegality, obviously a religion proscribed by the
state was illegal. But the law of states, the Christians
claimed, does not have the authority of the law of God,
as the pagan philosophers themselves agree. Here the
concept of the law of nature was invoked to justify civil
disobedience. The charges of immorality were branded as
simply not true. On the contrary the Christian communities by their deportment flared like beacons in the black-
ness of the pagan world.

What of the obscurantism of the Christians? Origen
replied that whereas the simple are not turned away, yet
they are not to be preferred. Athenagoras retorted that
good deeds are a sounder defense than subtle arguments.
But this was to abandon the encounter on the intellectual
front. This Origen would not do. He deduced the sincerity
of the first disciples from their willingness to endure
death for the Gospel. Deceived they might have been but
deceivers they were not. Their integrity was made evident
in that they recorded the embarrassing. Had they been
the inventors of fiction would they have mentioned that
Peter denied his Lord and that all of the disciples fled?
Here we have a type of reasoning tellingly revived in
modern times in defense of the historicity of Jesus, namely
that the Gospels contain a considerable number of statements about Jesus which went counter to the views that
had come to prevail in the early church and therefore
could never have been invented at the time when the
Gospels were written. The reply to the political charges

against the early Christians will be considered in a later section.

Rival Religions. *A. The Mystery Religions.* (*See Document 4, I.*) Thus far we have been concerned with the emergence of Christianity as a new religion in the face of opposition from both Jews and Gentiles. The persecution, to be sure, was not continuous and in the third century there were, roughly speaking, two periods of fifty years each of relative peace for the Church, from 200-250 and then, after the brief persecution of Decius, from 250 to approximately 300. Still the threat was never lifted. The quality of the Church was purified by the danger in a period when there was little temptation to join the Church for wealth, power, or prestige. Persecution, if not too drastic, welds a community. This was the general result of the Roman persecutions of Christianity, although on two occasions the attack was sufficiently drastic to cause huge defections.

The greater danger to the cohesion of the Church came from other religions which competed for converts and more insidiously corrupted Christianity in case members of these cults came over to the Church and tried to incorporate their own ideas into Christian theology.

These religions were of two types: Mystery religions and Gnosticism. They are examples of the nature religions and contemplative religions to which reference has already been made. The Mysteries—so called from the Greek word "mysterion," which means secret, applied to them because their rites were open only to initiates—discovered the evidence of the divine in the processes of nature and particularly in the dying and the rising of the seasons. The religious myth was first of all an explanation of the seasons. Vegetation dies because the god is dead and revives because the god is risen. The resurrection of nature in the spring means fertility for plants and animals. For that reason all these myths have a sexual element. Almost invariably there is a male and a female deity. The one dies; the other aids in the restoration to life. For example, we have in Babylon, Tammuz, the male who dies, and Ishtar, the female; in Syria, Adonis and Astarte; in Asia Minor, Attis and Cybele; in Egypt, Osiris and Isis. The relationship is reversed in the case of Eurydice who dies to be restored by Orpheus. In the myth of Persephone, the restorer is the mother, Ceres, whereas Pluto is the ravisher. The Mithraic cult lacked a goddess.

These myths were at the same time religions because the believer was to share in the experience of the god. Through identification the mortal put on immortality, became god and shared with the redeemer god the blessedness beyond the grave. There were various devices for achieving this identification. One was to eat the god. The assumption was that the god inhabited an animal or a fish which would be killed and eaten with the utmost haste before the divine spirit escaped. This practice developed into a more decorous sacramental meal of bread and fish. Another way was by being sprinkled with the blood of an animal, a bull or a goat. Being washed in the blood of the bull was called the *taurobolium,* and of the goat, the *crinobolium.* Although the Mysteries over the centuries refined their rites, these practices survived in all their crudity into the Christian era. Union with the god was sought by emotional excitation stimulated sometimes by the experience of sex. Hence sacred prostitution.

Inebriation as applied to religious experience was at first more than a metaphor. Orgiastic dances to the point of vertigo made of the initiate and enthusiast in the literal sense of the word which is derived from the two Greek words "en" and "theos" meaning "in god." More refined methods included the use of religious processions and drama. The rape and rescue of Persephone, for example, were annually portrayed at the cave at Eleusis. Again, music made its appeal from the lyre of Orpheus.

This type of religion, one observes, makes use of all that is sensory as an avenue to the divine. God is found by way of the mouth, the eye, and the ear. The sacred meal, the gorgeous procession, the cantata induced exaltation of feeling. Thus sacraments, art, and music in religion are derived from this attitude toward the world of sense. Obviously the primitive rites were crude. Yet this whole approach in more sublimated form has exercised a persistent lure by which Christianity has been alternately attracted and repelled.

The Mystery cults made a great appeal because they offered salvation from sorrow and death, because they were universal, accepting men of every race and social class (slaves were not excluded), because the units were small and intimate, because the invariability of the seasons afforded ground for religious certainty. Cicero said that the Eleusinian mysteries had conferred upon mankind the greatest boon of the blessed hope of immortality.

The Mysteries would find in Christianity some elements unintelligible and uncongenial, such as the creation of the world, the incarnation of god in man, the voluntary dying of Christ, and the doctrine of sin and grace. Other elements would be all too intelligible: the resurrection, the rebirth, and the sacraments. Converts from the Mystery religions to Christianity would tend to think of the resurrection as the rebirth of a nature god, and Easter would become a fertility rite centering on eggs and rabbits. The Lord's Supper would be an actual consuming of the flesh and blood of the god. Jesus would be the only god except for the goddess, the Virgin Mary. Against such misreadings the Church was required to be on guard. Her general principle was one of intransigence at the core and flexibility at the periphery. The cardinal doctrines of the faith could not be recast, but there was no objection to setting the celebration of the birth of Jesus on December 25, the winter solstice on Julian calendar, the birthday of the sun god Mithras. By setting the Christian festival on the same day, converts from Mithraism were preserved from relapsing on that occasion.

B. Gnosticism. Gnosticism was much more insidious because there were very gifted minds, such as Valentinus, who sought to recast Christianity into its mould. Gnosticism is a religion of contemplation which seeks God by the way opposite to that of the Mysteries. The sensory world is not regarded as an aid but rather as an impediment to religion, and the body as a clog. The roots of this view go back to Orphism which curiously has a myth like that of the Mysteries, for Orpheus seeks to reclaim Eurydice from the world of shades. He does so by the most refined of sensory means, music. But this myth is not so much of the essence of Orphism as the fragment in which the soul says, "I am a son of earth and of the starry heaven." Here is the dualism which enters the Platonic tradition, pitting against each other soul and

body and making of religion a way of escape, a rising
above the trammels of the flesh until the soul is wrapt in
ecstasy, discarding the visible for the invisible, absorbed
into the being of the ineffable One. Gnosticism, following
this fundamental pattern, assumes that salvation is by
way of *gnosis,* which is not so much knowledge as insight
and illumination. There are stages on the way, corresponding to the body, the soul, and the spirit of man.

Gnosticism was a religion. It was also a cosmology and
had an intellectual concern, as the Mysteries did not, to
explain the origin of the world, of man, and of his present
plight, and his way of deliverance. The Gnostic mytholo-
gies vary in detail and our knowledge of them is limited
because the number of Gnostic works to survive is small.
We have the *Pistis Sophia,* the *Hymn of the Robe of
Glory,* the *Hermetic Literature,* and the newly discovered
Gospel of Truth of Valentinus. (*See Document 4, II, A.*)
For the rest we are dependent upon the unsympathetic
accounts in the Church Fathers. Despite their variations
the Gnostic systems assume at the beginning, if one can
use the term "beginning" in a realm devoid of time, a
great abyss of being.—How different from the Hebrew
picture of the transcendent God!—This being is not
static but self-diffusive and wells up, throwing off emanations, perchance seven, the hebdomad, or eight, the og-
doad, and so on. The Gnostics, like the Pythagoreans,
were very fond of number symbolism. The sum of the
emanations constitutes the Pleroma, the fullness of the
Godhead. These emanations explain in part the transition
from the ultimate abyss to the cosmos. But of themselves
they are not a sufficient explanation. In addition to the
emanations there was a fall. Wisdom, herself one of the
emanations, was consumed with an inordinate curiosity
to understand the mystery of the process and in her dis-
tress cast off the matter out of which our world was
fashioned by a semi-divine figure, the Demiurge. The importance of this myth is that the fall precedes creation
which is therefore evil. The visible world is evil. Life in
the world and the flesh is evil. The Gnostic myth places
a stigma on the created world. That was why Tertullian
said that had he to choose between Gnosticism and the
Mysteries he would elect the Mysteries because they do

not vilify creation. But although Wisdom was responsible for the fall, she seeks to deliver man from the fall and thus becomes a redeeming principle.

Gnosticism blended freely with any of the religions of the empire, recasting them into its own form. There was, for example, a gnosticized Judaism achieved by a reversal of values. In the book of Genesis God saw that what He had created was good but when the Gnostics took over the story, the creator God became the evil Demiurge and the fall of Adam and Eve was represented rather as a redemption. The serpent was a saviour because he told Adam and Eve to eat of the tree of the Knowledge, that is the *gnosis* of good and evil. All those in the Old Testament who followed Yahweh such as Abraham and Noah were bad, and those who rebelled against Him such as Cain and Kore were good. Thus the entire scale of values was completely reversed.

When Gnosticism blended with Christianity the role of the redeemer fell of course to Christ. But since matter is evil He could not have had a material body. God did not become flesh. The incarnation had of necessity to be denied. God did not suffer in the flesh, and the suffering of Jesus on the cross could not have been real. His life in the body was only an appearance. He *seemed* to be. Hence the Greek word meaning "to seem," *dokeo,* was applied to this view which is called docetic.

Such a fundamental perversion of the faith the Church could not tolerate. To borrow the birthday of Mithras for the birthday of Jesus was innocuous, but to say that the creator of heaven and earth was a Demiurge, that God in Christ did not come in the flesh, that Jesus was not a real man—this was insufferable. The great fight of the early Church was not for the divinity but for the humanity of Jesus.

The Consolidation of the Church through Scripture and Episcopacy. But how could one prove that these Gnostics were wrong? The first and most obvious way was to appeal to the writings that came from the age of the Apostles. There were the books of our present New Testament consisting of the major letters of Paul and the epistle to the Hebrews, the pastoral letters ascribed to Paul and addressed to Timothy and Titus, the letters ascribed to Peter, James, Jude, and John, the Four Gospels, the Book of Acts and the Book of Revelation. But why were these books and only these to be regarded as genuine and authoritative? There were other books in circulation and highly esteemed in the churches, such as the Shepherd of Hermas, and the other writings known as the Apostolic Fathers, though actually they belonged to the sub-apostolic age. The Muratorian Fragment (named for the discoverer Muratori) (*see Document No. 5, I*), dating from about A.D. 180 shows us what books were coming to be placed in the first category and what in the second in Christian esteem.

One principle was that a book to be authoritative must have been written by an apostle or a companion of an apostle. But this test in practice was not decisive. For example, there was the Gospel of Peter. The congregation at Antioch came to Bishop Serapion and asked him if they might use this book. Certainly they might. Anything by Peter would of course be acceptable. The bishop made his reply, however, before he had examined the book. When he came to read it he discovered Gnostic elements and had to inform his flock that it simply could not be by Peter who would never have written anything of this sort. Thus, in this instance, we see that the authority of the book did not determine the truth of the doctrine, but the falsity of the doctrine disclosed the spuriousness of the book.

Moreover, if a book had the right doctrine a way could be found to attribute it to an apostle or a companion of an apostle. No one today would contend that the second epistle of Peter was actually written by Peter and there is grave doubt likewise with regard to the first epistle, but his name was attached to both of them. This practice was not deemed dishonest, for antiquity had little interest in literary ownership. The Jews assigned all law to Moses, all Psalms to David, and all wisdom to Solomon. Similarly, the Christians assigned the valuable books to the Apostles. This they appear to have done in the case of John's Gospel. Curiously, it was known and quoted early in the second century but never mentioned as by John until around the year 180. The assumption is that apostolic authorship was discovered for the gospel because it was so powerful a weapon with which to combat the Gnostics and others in error.

On the basis of value rather than of authorship the Christian congregations gradually selected our present New Testament. The process was nearly complete by the year 250 and it may be said to have been definitely closed by the festal letter of Athanasius in 367.

But the question of what is truth was in many crucial instances not thereby settled. The Gnostics had an insidious way of accepting New Testament writings and placing upon them their own interpretations. The Apostle Paul had talked about the fullness of the Godhead. What was this, if not the *pleroma* of the Gnostics? The apostle spoke of babes in Christ. This was a reference to the first stage in the Gnostic way.

How little the Scriptures as such sufficed was evident in the case of Marcion. (*See Document No. 4, II, B.*) He was and he was not a Gnostic. He had no cosmology like the Gnostics, but he did take a docetic view of Christ and considered the world evil and ascribed the creation to the Demiurge. For this reason Marcion rejected the whole of the Old Testament. Yahweh, he said, was a fickle, resentful, malevolent deity, a God of repulsive sacrifices and deeds of blood. The God of the New Testament was a God of grace and loving kindness. The difference, Marcion said, is seen in that the Apostle Paul said, "Let not the sun go down upon your wrath" whereas Joshua kept the sun up until his wrath went down. The Old Testament must therefore be rejected. As for the New Testament, Marcion was the first to draft a canon, that is an accepted list of New Testament books. For him they consisted of the letters of Paul and the Gospel of Luke. Perhaps he knew no more, but at any rate these, he said, had themselves been corrupted by the introduction of favorable references to the Old Testament. All such allusions he undertook to excise. He was the first Biblical critic.

The Church was thereby driven to decide whether or not to retain the Old Testament. The trouble was that it enjoined the observance of the Jewish law which the Christians rejected. The conclusion was to abandon the law but to keep the book and to allegorize whatever was not retained in practice. As for the New Testament, the text was stoutly defended. Yet all of this controversy disclosed that disputes could not be settled simply by appeal to books, doubly so because the Gnostics appealed to an oral tradition independent of books claiming that Christ and the apostles had committed secret teachings to favorite followers who had in turn transmitted these communications to the Gnostics. This claim raised questions as to the genuineness, the validity, and the source of tradition.

The question was answered in almost identical terms by Irenaeus and Tertullian. (*See Document No. 5, II, C.*) They said in effect, "Grant that the apostles confided to chosen disciples some teachings beyond those which found their place in the written record. To what disciples then would such a precious deposit have been committed? Would not the apostles have entrusted their treasure to those disciples to whom they committed the churches, and would not these disciples in turn have passed on the secrets to their successors in office? If then we would discover the extra-biblical tradition we should have recourse to those churches where it is possible to trace an unbroken line of succession in the bishopric back to the apostles. Nowhere can this be better done than at Rome where the Church was organized "by the two glorious apostles, Peter and Paul, and whose successors can be named to our own time: Linus, Anacletus, Clement, Evaristus, Sixtus, who was sixth after the apostles, Telesephorus, Hyginus, Pius, Anicetus and Soter."

This composite statement brings together for the first time three separate strands, namely episcopacy, that is the governance of the churches, each by a single head rather than by a board of elders; apostolic succession; and the primacy of Rome. Each of the three had emerged in the course of a long development and each calls for a word.

Church polity in the period of the New Testament exhibited variety with anticipations of the three forms later to be advanced with exclusive claims: congregationalism was evident in that each congregation was an independent unit not subject to more than advisory control from any higher body; presbyterianism appeared in the council of Jerusalem, described in Acts 15, which passed decrees "for to keep" and certainly looked for acquies-

cence on the part of the churches; at the same time the
Apostle Paul in his oversight of the new congregations
exercised the functions of the later diocesan bishop. The
term "bishop" in the early period was not applied to a
general superintendent but to the pastor of a local congregation. His status and functions cannot be precisely
determined in the days of the Apostle Paul because of the
confusion which surrounds the word elder. Sometimes it
means only an elderly person and sometimes designates
an office. What then was the relationship of this office
to that of the bishop? We read in Acts 19 that Paul summoned the elders of Ephesus and exhorted them to be
good bishops of their flocks. Some historians have therefore assumed that the church had a collegiate form of
government and that the term "bishop," which literally
means overseer, may have referred to the one who, at a
given time, presided at the Lord's Supper.

Early in the second century all such ambiguity had disappeared in the churches of Asia Minor. The correspond-
ence of Ignatius of Antioch makes plain that he was the
single bishop of Antioch in Syria and in his judgment no
rite of the church was valid apart from the bishop. (*See
Document No. 5, II B.*) The authority of the bishops
was, however, not derived from the doctrine of apostolic
succession. Ignatius grounded his authority on the Holy
Spirit using him as a mouthpiece. Polycarp, Bishop
of Smyrna, exhorted the Philippians to guard the tradition without any suggestion that it was lodged with the
bishop or that he himself stood in succession of the
apostles. The doctrine of apostolic succession first appeared at Rome (*see Document No. 5, II, A*) where
Clement, around A.D. 95, writing on behalf of the Roman
congregation, sought to allay dissension in the church at
Corinth by insisting on obedience to the bishops because
the bishops were from the apostles as the apostles were
from Christ and Christ from God.

In the claims advanced by Irenaeus and Tertullian,
episcopacy and apostolic succession are combined and
with them is associated the third point of the primacy of
Rome because Rome was founded by the two apostles
Peter and Paul. And after them an unbroken line in the
bishopric could be traced to their own days. One observes

that Irenaeus and Tertullian do not agree in their lists. For Irenaeus, Clement was the third heir to the Apostles but for Tertullian, the first. A graver difficulty is that this Clement in his epistle, above mentioned, makes no reference whatever to his own office as bishop and speaks as if bishops and elders were interchangeable, suggesting that Rome throughout the first century had the collegiate form of government. One notes also that if Sixtus was the sixth, as in the list of Irenaeus, then Peter was not the first. This is true also in the only other early lists of the bishops of Rome, the one by Hegesippus and the other in a source employed by Eusebius. In fact, the earliest clear statement that Peter was the first bishop of Rome is not found until the year 354 when it appears in the Liberian catalog. Those who accept this statement as valid explain the other accounts to mean that a distinction was drawn between Peter the apostolic Bishop and those bishops who followed, so that Sixtus was not the sixth bishop but the sixth in the line of the bishops after Peter. At any rate, the tradition is early that Peter died as a martyr in Rome. This is implied in the letter of Clement.

By A.D. 180, then, the view had come to prevail that pre-eminently in Rome, though also in a number of other churches such as Antioch and Ephesus, an unbroken chain of bishops reached back to the apostles and to them one should turn for the tradition.

But what was to be done if the Scriptures disagreed, if the apostles disagreed, if the successors of the apostles, the bishops, also disagreed? This situation arose in connection with the celebration of Easter. One question was when did Jesus die and rise from the dead? The chronology of John's gospel places the crucifixion on the fourteenth day of the Jewish month Nisan. Hence the party preferring this day was called *Quartodeciman* from the Latin word meaning the fourteenth. The other three gospels have the fifteenth. The churches of Asia Minor, following the lead of Ephesus, assumed to have been the scene of the final labors of the Apostle John, followed his gospel. The bishops of the area, including the great Polycarp, were Quartodeciman. The church of Rome followed the first three gospels and Anicetus, the bishop of Rome, disputed the question with Polycarp though in a tolerant spirit. Other questions also were involved. What was to be celebrated? The death or the resurrection of Christ? Those who used the fourteenth of Nisan were commemorating the crucifixion. Rome preferred to celebrate the resurrection. But should then the observance follow the day, that is Sunday, regardless of the date, or the date regardless of the day? Rome voted for the day. And should one employ the Jewish chronology at all, as the Asiatic churches were doing, and not rather the Julian calendar as Rome preferred? The dispute became acute under Bishop Victor about A.D. 180 because a congregation of Asiatics in Rome observed the Asian practice with the result that some of the Roman congregations were feasting while others were fasting. How should the question be resolved? The Gospels diverged. The bishops of the great apostolic churches disagreed. One might have argued that the Roman tradition was superior because Rome had the two apostles, Peter and Paul, whereas Asia had only one, the Apostle John. We do not know what arguments were used by Victor. We do know that he excommunicated first the Asiatic group in Rome and then the Asian churches. Where scriptures failed, where apostolic succession failed, arbitrary authority was invoked. Precisely when the excommunication was lifted we do not know. At any rate the dispute subsided and the Roman practice prevailed.

The tendency to exhalt authority and institutionalism was further augmented by the rise of Montanism, named from Montanus, a Phrygian bishop, who kept alive and exaggerated the New Testament emphasis on the Spirit. For the Apostle Paul all of the offices in the church were gifts of the Spirit. Wisely the Apostle included among the gifts of the Spirit the gift of discerning the spirits. In other words, some were providentially endowed with the ability to tell who had the Spirit. But who then would be able to determine who had the gift of determining who had the Spirit? Montanus affirmed that he was "spirit and word and power." He claimed the Spirit also for women and was accompanied by prophetesses. This was in accord with a reference in the book of Acts to the daughters of Philip who prophesied (Acts 21:9) but in disaccord with the word of the Apostle Paul who said that women should be silent in church (I Cor. 14:34). Paul's word had increasingly prevailed. The Spirit revealed to Montanus that the Lord would soon appear whereas other Christians were advancing the date of his return by several hundred years. Montanus, during the interval of waiting, demanded abstinence from marriage and rigid fasting. The churches at large perceived that the Spirit can get out of hand and they tended therefore to stress the tradition and to build up the authority of church officers. So intense was the feeling against the Montanists that when they and the orthodox were placed in the arena, they would separate themselves to opposite corners, dying for the same Lord, but not willing to be eaten by the same beasts.

Church Discipline. The government of the Church was further challenged and in the end strengthened by the disputes which arose over the exercise of discipline. Who should determine what sins excluded from the fellowship of the Church and on what terms readmission might be obtained? A series of practical cases pointed up the issues and led to the formulation of the Church's teaching and practice.

The early Church made a distinction between sins with reference to their enormity. The three chief sins were apostasy, fornication, including adultery, and bloodshed. Could these sins be forgiven by God and if so, should they be forgiven by the Church? All Christians were clear that to the unbaptized, God would forgive any sin but since baptism washed away all previous sins, what would happen if a major sin were committed after baptism? The heathen in this respect had an advantage because for them the gates of mercy were forever open. The Christians ran a grave risk by using up baptism. For that reason some chose to wait until their deathbeds in order that the roster of their sins might be complete. Constantine did this and Tertullian advised waiting at least until after marriage by which the character is formed.

But most Christians were baptized following conversion and Tertullian is our first witness to the practice of infant baptism. Could such Christians obtain a second forgiveness? Through martyrdom they could, for this was the baptism of blood corresponding to the baptism of water. But could forgiveness be granted to those who had failed the test of martyrdom? This question is raised in the book of Hermas written in Rome about the middle of the second century. What should be the treatment of those who had denied the Lord in the persecutions. The conclusion of Hermas was that the Lord would grant one more chance and would forgive those who repented with a whole heart. (*See Document No. 6, I.*) But the teaching of Hermas did not meet with general acceptance and a century went by before the Church was ready to re-admit the lapsed.

In the meantime the question of sexual offense became acute. Bishop Callistus of Rome, about A.D. 220, ruled that the Church would forgive and readmit to fellowship those who were thus guilty. Tertullian roundly denounced such laxity. (*See Document No. 6, II, A.*) From his protest one observes that the authority of the Bishop of Rome was not automatically received even by one who had done so much to exhalt it. Another ruling by Callistus shocked the rigorists in that he allowed Christian women of the aristocracy to form monogamous unions with men beneath them in social rank—even with slaves —on a basis which legally constituted concubinage. The reason was that the number of women in the higher social levels exceeded that of the men. The Church desired that marriages be kept within the fold. These women were unwilling to marry slaves because they would take the status of their husbands, but this change of social status would not occur if the union did not have the full legal status of marriage. The Church regarded these unions as real marriages, since they were monogamous and for life. This is the first instance in which church law diverged from civil law. But the Puritans saw here a concession if not to lust, at least to pride. (*See Document No. 6, II, B.*)

Callistus defended his procedure on the ground that he was the successor of Peter to whom Christ committed the keys of the kingdom, with authority to bind and loose on earth as in heaven. Callistus is the first Bishop of Rome to cite this Petrine passage. His policy was further undergirded by a theory of the Church which, for him, was not a community of saints but an assembly of

saved sinners, like Noah's Ark which included not only
the clean beasts but also the unclean. Again he described
the Church as the field in which the Lord commanded
that the tares be left to grow together with the wheat.
Callistus here formulated the theory of the Church as an
ark of salvation within which the moral offender should
be treated leniently, since as long as he remained within
the ark he might be saved even though he were unclean,
whereas if he were cast out he would be irretrievably lost
even though he were clean. With Callistus the exclusion
of penitent sexual offenders ceased and the Roman practice became universal.

The treatment of the lapsed came to a head after the
persecution of Decius in A.D. 250, during which the majority of the congregations sometime fell away. When the
danger was past they desired to be readmitted. (*See Document 6, III, A-D.*) They could urge that in their hearts
they had not denied and that they still loved the Lord,
but they could plead urgent reason for their restoratism.
Callistus' theory of the Church had received more explicit
formulation by Bishop Cyprian of Carthage who said,
"Outside of the Church there is no salvation. He cannot
have God for his father who has not the Church for his
mother." How imperative, then, that the lapsed be restored and how appropriate that the confessors, that is
those who had endured torture without yielding and were
still alive when the edict of persecution was rescinded,
should be the ministers of magnanimity! These confessors
began to issue indiscriminate pardons, for example, "to
Lucius and his friends." Two or three dozen could be
readmitted under that rubric. Bishop Cyprian protested.
He was in a very embarrassing position, however, because
he had withdrawn during the persecution. Eight years
later, when the test was renewed, he stayed and suffered.
On this occasion, to impede the confessors was delicate,
but to leave them entire freedom would wreck all discrimination. Cyprian pointed out that some of the lapsed
had rushed to sacrifice, some had succumbed only after
severe torture, some had not sacrificed at all but had paid
a fee for certificates which affirmed that they had sacrificed, although the authorities well knew that they had
not. Each case should be examined individually and rules

should be devised for graded penance in accord with the enormity of the offense. All of this should be administered *by the bishop.* The sum of it all was that the lapsed could be forgiven. Tertullian against Callistus had argued, "If we do not forgive the lapsed, shall we forgive adulterers?" Cyprian argued, "Since we forgive adulterers, shall we exclude the lapsed?" At a less determinable point the bars went down also for homicide. All sins, then, could be forgiven, both by God and by the Church and the decision should rest with the bishop. Against this conclusion schisms arose in Africa, Egypt, and in Rome. The latter was headed by Novatian who came to have an extensive and long-continued following. The rigorists held that the Church is less an ark of Noah than a city upon a hill to give light by example to the world. Theirs was the moralistic theory of the Church.

The Creed. But what was meant by being in the Church? The answer was that to be in the Church meant to be admitted to her sacraments, particularly to the supper of the Lord. Excommunication meant exclusion from communion, but no one could be admitted to communion who did not believe what the Church believed. And whereas on some matters the Church might be accommodating, yet as to the core there must be intransigence, otherwise Christianity would have been dissipated in the mingling of religions. What then was the Church's faith? Affirmations of faith abound in the New Testament as for example when the Apostle Paul speaks of "Christ who died, or rather has been raised from the dead, who is on the right hand of God, who also makes intercession for us" (Rom. 8:34). Converts in the early church were given a period of instruction at the end of which they recited a creed. At baptism they were asked a series of questions concerning their faith. Out of such statements the Apostle's Creed arose. In its primitive form it is called the Old Roman Symbol. The form we see today is a revision elaborated in southern Gaul between the seventh and the ninth centuries and subsequently adopted at Rome. (*See Documents No. 5, III, A, B, C.*)

In the definition of her faith the Church needed succinct formulae which would both comprise the essentials of the New Testament teaching and guard against errors.

The implications of these affirmations called for fuller exposition with an eye to philosophical as well as theological questions. The Christian Fathers became the heirs and transmitters of the Greek philosophical tradition. And even those who, like Tertullian, spoke scornfully of the wisdom of the Greeks, declaring that Jerusalem had nothing to do with Athens, yet drew heavily from Stoicism. Christian theology has been perpetually strained by the tension between its Hebraic and Hellenic ingredients. The Church Fathers, while drinking from the well of Jacob, did not disdain the cisterns of the Gentiles. In general, the Greek Fathers, such as Justin and especially the Alexandrians, Clement of Alexandria and Origen, were more hospitable to the Greek tradition than were the Latins and particularly the north Africans like Tertullian, Cyprian, and even Augustine.

In their theology they sought to include the Hebraic view of God as a person, marked by intelligence, will, and love, with a view derived from the philosophical tradition of God as the ultimate abyss of being who can be described only in negative terms: immeasurable, incomprehensible, inconceivable. They asserted, of course, with the Jews that God is one and the Lord of the universe. The greatest problem was to explain Christ and his relationship to God. The Church was absolutely clear that Christ was a man. The very doctrine of the incarnation was that God became man, and if Christ was not really man then there was no incarnation. He was man in real flesh and not in appearance. He was truly born, truly suffered, truly died as Ignatius strenuously insisted. But he was certainly no ordinary man. He was a revealer of God. Ignatius has a picture of God as silence until in Christ He spoke. To reveal God, Christ must have known God. The gospel says, "No one knows the Father save the Son" (Matt. 11:27). To know God He must have pre-existed with God. He had saved man from guilt through the propitiation of sin and had saved man from sinning by way of his moral example. He had saved man also from sinfulness, changing his nature into that of a new creature, and had saved man from death by the resurrection from the dead. To serve as a moral example he must have been a genuine human being subject to man's temptations. But to achieve the forgiveness of sin and to confer upon man a new nature he must have been, in some sense, God.

The Church Fathers at first laid hold of concepts already at hand, the Wisdom of the Hebrews and *logos* of the Greeks. Christ was the Wisdom of God. The difficulty here, however, was that Wisdom had been hypostasized into a second god, whereas all the Christians were agreed that Christ was not sufficiently distinct from God to be regarded as a second god. He was then identified with the *logos* of the Stoics, the immanent reason of the universe. Here the difficulty was that the *logos* was simply God in one mode of his existence, and this would identify Christ too closely with God. Both explanations appeared among the early Christians. One made Christ a subordinate divine being. This was called dynamic monarchianism, both terms being used in their original Greek sense. Monarchianism referred to the oneness of God. Dynamic referred to a special *dynamis* or power resident in Jesus which made him more than man but left him less than God. The other view, that Christ was simply a mode of God's activity, was called modalistic monarchianism.

The Church Fathers rejected both views and sought a middle ground. Christ was not a second god. He was not a mode of God's activity. The Son was distinct from the Father but there were not two gods. By and by the Spirit was brought into the picture and what applied to the Son applied largely also to the Spirit.

A solution was found by way of the concept of being or substance, in Greek *ousia,* in Latin *substantia.* Valentinus had said that Wisdom is of the same substance as God, *homoousios.* The Orthodox Christians eventually adopted this term to express the relationship of Christ to God. In Latin it was consubstantial. Tertullian first formulated the doctrine of the Trinity. The Son and the Spirit, he said, participate in the being of God. They are of one being or substance with the Father. There are thus three persons and one substance. But Tertullian leaned to modalism when he said that the differentiation is in accord with dispensations, but again to subordinationism when he said the Son is a portion of God, and in the end God will be all in all. Tertullian believed that the

Son came into being only at the incarnation and was
therefore not eternal. But Origen asserted the eternal,
timeless generation of the Son. Yet for him generation
implied subordination. Thus during the first three centuries the main lines of Christian doctrine were adum-
brated, leaving ambiguities for future clarification.

The heretics made their contribution to the development, both negatively and positively. The Orthodox affirmations had to be so couched that they would exclude
the heretical. And it may well be that the emphasis in
the creeds only upon the birth, suffering, and death in
the earthly life of Christ was due to the desire to refute
the Gnostics on these points. Positively, Valentinus contributed the word "homoousios" and Tertullian's affirmation of the doctrine of the Trinity, in which the Spirit
was one of the three, may have been due to the influence
of the Montanists whom in later life he joined. One
heretic retarded the adoption of the word "homoousios"
by the Orthodox through his use of the term in an unac-
ceptable sense. This was Paul, Bishop of Samosata around
A.D. 370. He combined modalistic and dynamic monarchianism. The *logos,* but not Jesus, was a mode of God's
activity and of one substance with God, *homoousios.* But
Jesus was a man of exceptional moral excellence who
was chosen by the *logos* for indwelling and thus was
adopted to be the Son of God. The condemnation of the
view of Bishop Paul rendered all of his terminology for
sometime suspect.

— 2 —

THE CHURCH AND SOCIETY

As to the attitude of the Christians toward society we have noted that Celsus accused them of irresponsibility and declared that if all men were as they, the empire would be overrun with lawless barbarians. A century earlier the Christians had been charged with hatred of the human race. The phrase was not spelled out by the historian Tacitus, but information from other sources enables us to conjecture with plausibility what he must have meant. The abstention of the Christians from the practices of their neighbors was much more extensive in pagan antiquity than in modern secularized society, because secularism compartmentalizes the spheres of religion and society. For a parallel to antiquity one needs to turn to the Orient before the recent revolutions. In old China a wall might be built across a street to impede the passage of demons; cooking was fraught with religious significance; and art portrayed religious themes. But in modern France or America there could be no clash over city planning, cuisine, or interior decoration because the religious connotations are gone.

In the early Church the Christians held aloof from society for two reasons: religious and moral. The first limited their participation in trades. (*See Document No. 7, II.*) Sculpture as such was possible but not for the making of idols. Gilding was possible, but again not if the object were an idol. Schools presented a problem because they taught the classics and the classics embodied the myths of the gods. Even hospitals were compromising because they existed under the patronage of Aesculapius. On moral grounds the Christians could not approve of abortion, infanticide, or the exposure of children. In

49

mixed marriages there might easily be quarrels over these points and for that reason such unions were discouraged by the Church, which, in consequence, became all the more a group apart. The exclusiveness did not cease with death, for Christians desired to be buried together and the Christian wife might thus be entombed apart from her husband. Bloodshed was abhorred by the Church. Therefore, of course, gladiatorial combats were condemned and the Christians could not witness them. Neither could they attend the theater where the performances were lewd and the faith might be ridiculed. Christians could assume no magisterial post that carried with it the possibility of passing a sentence of death. War was also prohibited to them. (*See Document No. 7, I.*)

Though in the world, the Christian was very definitely not of the world. (*See Document No. 7, II.*) The Christian apologists sought to allay the distrust of their neighbors by insisting that though not of the world they were definitely in the world and that they dissociated themselves from so many activities through no aversion to mankind. Tertullian stressed all that the Christians would do in common with the pagans, "We do not go to your feasts but we patronize your industries. We do not buy laurel crowns but we buy flowers. We do not buy incense for temples but we do for burial. We do not contribute to the temples but we give more for alms than do you. We improve business in that we do not defraud. You really lose by putting us to death because if we are Christians we are good men; if we are not good men we are not Christians." (*Apology 42.*)

Political Attitudes. Christian attitudes may now be considered more specifically under the rubrics of the political, the domestic, and the economic.

As for the political, the Christians condemned the emperor but not the empire. So long as the emperor claimed to be God he was "the abomination of desolation." But the empire was never identified with Antichrist. In his second letter to the Thessalonians, Paul had warned his readers not to expect the immediate return of the Lord because first must come "a man of sin setting himself forth in the temple as God." But, said the Apostle, there is "a power which restrains." The early Church identified the "man of sin" with the deified emperor and the "power which restrains" with the empire. Of course the empire did not restrain the emperor. The empire restrained that chaos with its wars and rumors of wars, which would precede the great *dénouement*. The Christians so appreciated the present order as to be in a strait whether to pray "come quickly, Lord Jesus" or *pro mora finis*, that is, for the delay of the end. The order of the empire, they realized, was of great advantage to the faith, since the freedom of the seas from pirates and of the roads from brigands facilitated the spread of the gospel.

At the same time, the attitude toward the government was cool. Already in the New Testament three views were apparent. The writings of Luke were the most favorable. He only noted the coincidence of the events in the life of Christ with the chronology of the empire, that is, the birth of Christ under Augustus, and the commencement of our Lord's ministry under Tiberius. In the book of Acts, Luke looked upon the empire as the protector of the Christians. The book of Revelation was the most hostile, written at the end of the first century in the reign of the persecutor, Domitian. Rome in this book was equated with Babylon, drunk with the blood of the saints. In between these two positions was the view of the Apostle Paul who said that the "powers that be are ordained of God and bear not the sword in vain to punish the bad and protect the good. For this reason the government should be obeyed not out of fear but out of conscience" (Romans 13, *condensed*).

These three New Testament positions reappeared in the early Church. The Lukan attitude of favor toward the empire was continued by eastern theologians who held that at the very same time God had made Augustus emperor He had sent Christ to save the world. Therefore, the empire and the Church might be regarded as two conjoint works of God for the salvation of mankind. The extreme hostility of the Book of Revelation recurred in a poem by Commodianus, who at the time of the last persecutions would have welcomed a Gothic invasion for the overthrow of the empire. The prevailing view was in line with a statement of the Apostle Paul that the powers

that be are ordained of God. But what, precisely, did
this statement mean for Christian participation in government? On that score, three positions emerged in later
Christian history. Some said that the powers, that is,
governments, were ordained of God because of sin and
their administration should be left to sinners. So spoke
the Anabaptists in the age of the Reformation. Others
said that, although in a Christian society government
would be unnecessary, yet in this present world of sin it
cannot be eliminated. Therefore, the Christian, even
though he has no need of it for himself, should nevertheless assume office so that justice may be the better administered. So spoke Luther. Others argued that since the
powers are ordained of God they must be good and the
Christian need feel no compunction about exercising them.
Such was the view of Calvin. The position of the early
Church was not so precisely defined, but the general
aloofness resembled that of the later Anabaptists. Origen,
for example, compared the state to a chain gang, doing
good work, though composed of criminals. Tertullian was
the most extreme in his statement that nothing is so alien
to the Christian as political life. Origen held that for the
Christian the Church offered the only sphere for activity.
But this was not without political significance because
the Church itself was a force of order creating a peaceableness within the framework of the external peace of
Rome. Though the Christian recognized the empire as
ordained of God and though the Christian prayed for the
emperor, yet the Christian himself could scarcely ever
become an emperor.

The Attitude Toward War. With regard to war,
Celsus, the pagan, writing around A.D. 180 had assumed
that no Christian would ever accept military service, and
Origen, the Christian, replying to him three quarters of
a century later, had accepted and justified such complete
abstention. As a matter of fact, however, we know that
at the very time of Celsus some Christians were enrolled
in the so-called "thundering legion" under Marcus
Aurelius. From then on the evidence that Christians
served in the army increases, though there is no reason
to believe that they were ever numerous. Only six definitely pre-Constantinian inscriptions on Christian tombs

indicate that the deceased was a Christian. Coincidently, the protest against Christian participation in war became audible and explicit. No Christian writer prior to the time of Constantine approved of Christian participation in warfare. The sepulchral inscriptions indicate that Christian soldiers were not excommunicated, but their presence in the ranks met with disfavor. (*See Document No. 7, I.*)

Some modern historians make a distinction between aversion to military service and aversion to warfare. They contend that the early Fathers were not pacifists, but discountenanced military service on several possible counts. First, on the assumption that the Lord Jesus would quickly return and Christians should not assist, by warfare, to maintain the order which he would destroy. But, as we have noted, the Christians were not too eager to have this order overturned and in the third century deferred the coming of the Lord for some three hundred years. Another contention is that the Christians would not fight for an empire which subjected them to persecution. This might indeed have been true under Decius but only for two years was persecution ever drastic and universal. The explanation chiefly favored is that the Christian fear of service in the army arose from the danger of idolatry because the deified emperor was the commander-in-chief of the army and the officers were required to conduct sacrifices at his altar. But this was true only of officers and not of privates, and the argument proves too much. If idolatry was unavoidable then the Church should have excommunicated every soldier. Since this was not done we may infer that idolatry was not unavoidable.

The primary reason for the objection to participation in warfare was the aversion to bloodshed which was counted, as we have seen, among the three deadly sins. Long after the Church had come to condone Christian participation in warfare he who killed in battle had still to do penance before being received again to communion. This objection to bloodshed was based on a feeling for the incompatibility of love and killing. All the Church Fathers stressed that Christians take literally the command of love their enemies. The wars of the Old Testament were such an offence that Marcion rejected the Old Testament, pointing out that Jesus stretched out his arms in suffering upon the cross for the redemption of mankind, whereas Joshua upheld the arms of Moses until his enemies were slaughtered. The Church Fathers, who did not reject the Old Testament, explained such wars either as characteristic of a dispensation now superseded or else by way of allegory. Origen interpreted the wars of Yahweh as battles against vice. The Holy Spirit, he was sure, would never have recorded these wars had they been real.

Certain differences of emphasis among the Fathers are apparent. The pacifism of Marcion was ascetic. He despised the body and could not approve of a struggle of body against body. Significantly, in him we find combined pacifism, vegetarianism, and celibacy. The pacifism of Tertullian was eschatalogical and legalistic. The Lord Jesus would soon come—Tertullian believed this even though he might pray for delay—and in the meantime the Lord Jesus by telling Peter to put up his sword had ungirt every soldier. The pacifism of Origen was more pragmatic. He believed that the winsome Lord Jesus, who had already taken captive the souls of men as no philosopher or general of antiquity had ever done, would continue his bloodless victories until Celsus' picture of a pagan, barbarian world inundating a Christian pacifist empire would be unthinkable. Celsus said, "If all men were like you Christians. . . ." Origen replied, "If all men were Christians, the barbarians would be Christians." He looked especially to the Church as a redemptive and cohesive force in society. Many of the Fathers held that the Church rather than the empire was the power that restrained the great chaos. The Church was the Garden of Eden restored.

There is validity, however, in the distinction between military service and participation in warfare. The point is not that the Church discountenanced military service and allowed warfare but rather the reverse. Military service was allowed, but warfare rejected. This appears in the Canons of Hippolytus (*See Document No. 7, II*) who said that a Christian might be a soldier provided he did not kill. This sounds fantastic but it was not so during the *Pax Romana,* when peace prevailed from Hadrian's Wall in Scotland to the Euphrates save for skirmishes on the frontier. Under such circumstances the army was engaged in police work, fire protection, road maintenance, and much of what we call public works. One could thus be a soldier for a lifetime and never take a life.

The pacifism of the early Church appears to have been to a degree geographical. Our first evidence of Christians in the army shows them to have been recruited from the eastern provinces near the Persian frontier, whereas all of the Church Fathers who discountenanced warfare came from the interior of the empire. Apparently where the danger was more acute the reservations were relaxed.

Another way of handling the problem was taking shape not along the lines of geographical but of vocational differentiation. This was suggested by Origen when he said the Christians would pray for the emperor and for his armies, though declining to participate. The implication was that the emperor and his forces did have a role in the economy of God but Christians had another calling. Then the distinction invaded the church and Eusebius in the age of Constantine could say that some Christians were called upon to be celibate, propertyless, and defenseless; whereas others might marry, engage in business, and serve in just wars.

Domestic Relations. With regard to domestic relations the Church very early defended matrimony and yet more highly esteemed virginity. The Apostle Paul led the way when he looked upon marriage as a concession. Because of the shortness of the time until the coming of the Lord, he would have preferred that the unmarried should remained unmarried, lest if married they become encumbered and less unreservedly committed to the Lord. But if there were those who could not restrain themselves, it were better that they should marry than be tormented. Here is the view of marriage as a *remedium peccati,* a remedy for sin (I Corinthians 7). But when the Lord did not come, Paul's eschatological disparagement of marriage took on an ascetic tinge. Virginity was esteemed as a higher state than marriage. By Marcion it was required of all Christians. And some held that married Christians should abstain from each other. Against Marcion the Church took a firm stand. Tertullian vigorously defended marriage. Monogamy should be the form, for if God had intended polygamy, he would have used more than one rib of Adam. Polygamy had been temporarily allowed to the patriarchs because at that time the population was sparse. Second marriages were not permissible unless the first partner died prior to the baptism of the survivor, for baptism which washes away all previous sins also disposes of previous spouses. Husband and wife, being united in spiritual partnership, should join together in prayer and in praise.

The Church very early forbade contraception. The matter came up in connection with the situation already described under Callistus, for some of the aristocratic women who formed concubinous marriages with slaves were loath to have children by them because the children would take the status of the father. The use of contraception to prevent children in these unions was discountenanced. One observes that the condemnation was directed against those who wished to avoid having families altogether.

The Attitude Toward Property and Slavery. With regard to property the Church never espoused a thoroughgoing communism of production and consumption. There was a sharing of goods and a drastic philanthropy for the benefit not only of fellow Christians but also of the heathen, especially in times of calamity. The care for widows and orphans, the ransoming of prisoners, and the support of the families of martyrs all came from the common chest. The Christians likewise established hostels throughout the empire where traveling fellow-believers might be entertained. Such activities required money and Clement of Alexandria defended wealth and property as the prerequisite for philanthropy. But he was the only one among the Fathers who said a good word for wealth. And, too, he had much in praise of poverty. The Shepherd of Hermas felt that the poor conferred a benefit upon the rich. Thus generosity began to degenerate into a good work for the earning of heavenly credit.

The whole attitude toward poverty provides a most interesting example of the way in which the Fathers appropriated ideas from the classical world and modified then in a Christian sense. (*See Document No. 7, IV.*) The Cynics in antiquity were the apostles of poverty. For them it was a device to achieve tranquility. He who has nothing can lose nothing. If he despoils himself he can never be despoiled. Let him therefore reduce to the minimum. When Diogenes saw a boy drinking out of his hands the sage smashed his cup saying, "How long have I carried superfluous baggage?" Art was condemned as superfluous. Undyed cloth provided warmth quite as well as the dyed. Why adorn a table with ivory? Wood is as strong. Why make vessels of gold and silver when earthenware will suffice? These themes appear in a passage in Pseudo Lucian. They reappear in the writings of several of the Church Fathers with the addition of references to the poverty of Christ. (*See Document No. 7, IV, A.*)

At the same time there was a difference. The Cynic motive was the attainment of tranquility; the Christian motive, preparation for martyrdom. "Will the neck that wears a necklace," exclaimed Tertullian, "bow before the ax of the executioner? Will the ankles adorned with bracelets submit to the pressure of the screw?" (*See Document No. 7, IV, B3.*) The Christian must eschew all luxury and all adornment of the body, partly because they excite lust but even more because they enervate the will to suffer for the Lord. The Fathers wrote many treatises in which they inveighed against the adornment of women and excoriated the use of rouge, dye, and wigs. If God wanted us to have colored clothes, why did he not make purple sheep? If we wear wigs, when the presbyter lays his hands upon our heads in blessing whose hair will he bless? Men also were not to be concerned about their appearance. Let them not pluck the hairs from their beards; "the hairs of your heads are all numbered" and to pull any out spoils God's count. Such injunctions regale the modern reader until he recalls that these folk confronted imminent death. By austere living they prepared themselves for dying.

Slavery was not abolished by the early Church, although the distinction between slave and free disappeared in the Christian community. Callistus, the Bishop of Rome, had been a slave; Felicitas, the martyr, was a slave girl. So, too, was Blandina at Lyon. Slavery was humanized but not abolished. The reason may well have been the expectation of the Lord's early return, for which reason it mattered little whether one were slave or free.

Also, slavery did not encompass the brutality that it did in America in modern times. Slavery in the Roman empire has been well described as an enforced introduction into Roman culture. In three generations a slave could pass to the status of the freedman and then to that of the free man. There was no color line and no cultural line. The slave was often superior to his master. All of which is not to say that slavery was a desirable or a desired status. Today we may wish that the Christian conscience had then declared itself against the institution, but a reform movement is not always capable of waging an offensive on all fronts. Curiously, war was then condemned but is still with us whereas slavery was then condoned and has since been abolished in Christian lands.

— 3 —

THE CHRISTIAN ROMAN EMPIRE

The Persecution of Diocletian and the Conversion of Constantine. The entire relationship of the Church to the world was profoundly altered when the world ceased to be hostile to the Church. When, under Constantine, Christianity came to be the favored religion of the empire, Christian aloofness naturally diminished. The discipline requisite for martyrdom was relaxed, and the aversion to military service well nigh disappeared. The affiliation of Church and state brought with it, however, a new sort of friction as each encroached upon the domain of the other. The divisions in the Church were injected into the life of the state and fissures in the social structure rent the Church. The cohesiveness which the early Fathers claimed to be the contribution of the Church to society was disrupted and the Church assisted the disintegration of the empire.

The transition of the Church from fire to favor was preluded by the last great incandescence of persecution. Before the toleration of Constantine came the final attempt at extermination by Diocletian. The basic reason for the persecution was that the religious problem of the empire had not been solved. There were really two problems: to find a cult in which all of the inhabitants of the empire could unite, and to enlist the aid of those divinities who would insure the success of Roman arms. Christianity was increasingly rendering the imperial cult obsolete as a universal rite. The Emperor Aurelian, about A.D. 270, turned to Mithraism instead. This was a fatuous gesture because the strength of Mithraism was in the army, and lay, therefore, on the frontiers where the army was situated. Christianity was dominant in the great urban centers of the interior. Aurelian might have known that the religion of the fringe could not supplant the religion of the core. Diocletian addressed himself more to the other problem of obtaining the favor of the gods of victory. He is claimed to have been instigated to attack the Christians by his associate Galerius. Both men, like Decius before them, were soldiers from the Danubian front. So, also, was Maximinus Daia, later the associate of Galerius. They represented the army in which there were few Christians. The pagans of the army were less and less of the old Roman stock because the ranks were progressively replenished by the enrollment of fugitive barbarians coming over the great rivers. When Rome was sacked by Alaric the Goth, the general who defended Rome was Stilicho the Goth. These barbarian heathen admired the gods of ancient Rome by whose protection her empire had come into being. They felt that the rites of these gods should be restored and Christians should be forced to comply.

The persecution of Diocletian commenced in the year 303 with an edict calling for the surrender of church buildings and copies of the Scriptures. A second edict imprisoned church officers. When the prisons were overcrowded a third edict sought to empty them by extracting a minimum compliance. The failure of this plan led to the fourth edict which demanded sacrifice on pain of death from all inhabitants of the empire. As in the time of Decius, the emphasis was not on the imperial cult, but on the worship of the ancient gods. The persecution ended in the year 305.

In that year Diocletian abdicated. He did so in accord with a plan for avoiding wars of succession by instituting orderly procedures. The empire was divided for purposes of administration into East and West, each under an Augustus, though not of equal rank. Each Augustus was assisted by a Caesar. In due time the Augusti were to retire and be succeeded by the Caesars. The plan was disrupted by Constantine, son of the Caesar in the West who died shortly after the abdication of Diocletian. Constantine set himself up as his father's successor thus putting the dynastic above the bureaucratic principle. Thereupon

Maxentius, son of the Augustus in the West, determined to succeed his father. Galerius, who followed Diocletian, recognized Constantine but not Maxentius whose father was not dead, and with the approval of the retired Diocletian appointed instead Licinius. In the meantime Maximinus Daia had become the Caesar to Galerius in the East. But Maximian, the father of Maxentius, and the original Augustus in the West, declined to withdraw. Wars of succession followed and lasted for some twenty years. There were at one time seven contestants for the empire. The rivals in the West and in the East reduced the aspirants to one for each region and these played off the finals. From the point of view of the history of the Church, the significance of this turmoil is that Christianity had assumed such political importance that every contestant sought to advance his prospect by persecuting or tolerating the faith, depending upon its strength in given localities. The protracted struggle tended to break down Christian aloofness to the empire and the army. For whereas the Christians ascribed a persecuting aspirant and his troops to Satan, they regarded a champion of the faith, on the other hand, as the Lord's Anointed. Hence, when Constantine conquered, after two decades, by the sign of the Cross, the Church had not too many reservations to overcome in order to regard him as the instrument of the Almighty.

The struggle was marked by strange turns. In the year 311, Galerius, the former persecutor, issued an edict of toleration on the grounds that persecution had not achieved its goal. (*See Document No. 8, I.*) Constraint was actually making for irreligion because it deterred the Christians from the practice of their own faith yet did not induce them to return to the religion of their ancestors. They were publicly worshiping no gods. In the eyes of the Romans the abandonment of religious practices was atheism in the form most menacing to the welfare of the state. Better that the Christians supplicate their own god than none. Some historians believe Galerius was persuaded on his deathbed to take this stand by Licinius, who aspired to the conquest of Asia Minor, the most heavily Christianized area of the empire.

The next year, that is 312, Constantine marched against

Maxentius who held Rome. On the journey Constantine is said to have had a vision of the Cross in the heavens and the inscription, "By this, conquer." The story of the vision was recorded only twenty-five years after the event. A contemporary said that Constantine had had a dream. Some in our day have wondered whether he had anything at all. They insist that there was no political expediency in embracing Christianity at this time because Maxentius was not a persecutor but only an arbiter between rival Christian factions in Rome. The possibility is overlooked that Constantine might have acted from considerations other than those of political expediency. He himself affirmed that he had had a conversion and had been brought to see that the god of the Christians is the true God. To worship the true God was of course deemed politically expedient but not in terms of terrestial calculations. Constantine believed in providence, and in one God who governs the affairs of men, and that this God had disclosed himself in power through the resurrection of Jesus Christ. One may indeed wonder why Constantine should have had a vision of the *Cross* since his piety centered not on the death but on the resurrection of Christ. The rule of the true God, he perceived, had been opposed by previous emperors but had been defended by the sufferings of the martyrs until vindicated by the sword of Constantine. The emperor was thus the successor of the martyrs. On his military standards he placed the monogram of the first letters of the word "Christ" in Greek: *chi, rho.* (☧ The Greek X represents our *CH,* and the Greek P represents our *R.*)

Having defeated Maxentius, Constantine temporarily divided the empire with Licinius along the lines of East and West. The religious policy upon which the two agreed at a meeting at Milan was promulgated in the so-called Edict of Milan in the eastern provinces in the year 313. (*See Document No. 8, II.*) This document by no means established Christianity as the religion of the empire: It was simply an edict of universal toleration. It was indeed an abandonment of the policy of one empire and one religion, for each person should now be free to follow whatever worship he desired, that "whatsoever Divinity dwells in heaven may be benevolent and propitious to us."

This was an attempt to enlist the favor of whatever gods there be. There is in it half a note of skepticism coupled with a resolve to take the least chances. Under the circumstances more could scarcely have been affirmed because Constantine was a Christian whereas his colleague Licinius, though ready to drop persecution, was still a pagan.

Constantine himself did not talk in such ambiguous terms. Writing shortly after his conversion to an official in Africa he urged that all consideration be given to the clergy in order that they be not diverted "from the service which is owed to the divinity, . . . since their conduct of the greatest worship towards the divinity will, in my opinion, bring immeasurable benefit to the commonwealth."

Constantine did not have an opportunity to extend his policy to the entire empire until his victory over Licinius in A.D. 324. In the meantime, Constantine had been moving continually toward a more favored position for the Church. Not that he was ever willing to proscribe paganism, nor did he renounce his position as *pontifex maximus,* even though he performed none of the offices of the pagan high priest. Symbols of sun worship passed over into his Christianity. Yet the Church was favored; her properties were restored, and many new churches built at imperial expense. Sunday was made a holiday, although it was referred to as the day of the sun rather than as the Lord's day. Curiously, in our time it is the Sun's Day in the northern lands, whereas in the Latin countries it is the Lord's Day—*dominica, domingo, dimanche.*

What Constantine expected from Christianity is not a matter of conjecture. He looked for favor in heaven and for cohesion on earth. The Church should be what the Fathers had boasted her to be, namely the cement of the empire. The policy of Constantine may well have had other aspects of which he was less explicitly aware. The history of the empire from Augustus to his own day had been marked by the barbarization of the army, the militarization of the state, and the divinization of the ruler. Christianity was a counterpoise against all of these tendencies. The barbarians who filtered into the army were not in the Church which, as we have noted, had its strength in the peaceful interior. In consequence, Constantine avowedly began to identify Christianity with old Rome and to associate paganism with the barbarians. As for the militarization of the state, the Christians, even though they largely abandoned their objection to warfare, certainly did not espouse militarization. The deification of the ruler, of course, ceased altogether. Constantine had to give up being a god. The dilemma regarding the extermination of Christianity, the secularization of the state, or the establishment of Christianity was at last resolved. The trend was toward the latter, even though, undeniably, this meant some measure of secularization for the state because the ruler was neither a god nor a priest but only a layman in the Christian Church. Still, as a layman he could play a dominate role. Constantine, on many occasions, functioned more significantly than a bishop.

The first Christian emperor and the Church started out with high hopes for each other. The Christian bishops, when invited to dine with the emperor, wondered whether the Kingdom of God had come or whether they dreamed. Bishop Eusebius of Caeserea, in an oration on Constantine, maintained that the day at last had come when Church and empire had discovered their ordained accord. (*See Document No. 8, III.*) The manifold demons which incited men to war had been subdued by Christ in the heavenly places while on earth Constantine had overcome the enemies of God. Now, as there was one God in heaven, so on earth there was one emperor, and the prophecy had been fulfilled that swords should be beaten into ploughshares.

But the empire and the Church were to be disillusioned very shortly. Constantine was the first to experience disappointment. The Church which he had regarded as cement for the empire proved to be nitroglycerine. One is tempted to make the generalization that where the state is powerful, Christianity is disruptive, but when the state is disorganized Christianity is cohesive. At any rate, in the eastern empire Christianity fomented and fostered divisions, whereas in the West, after the barbarian invasions and in early Russia, Christianity was the builder of civilization.

The Donatist Controversy. Constantine's first disillusionment came in the West after his victory over Maxentius. Controversy had begun in Africa. The Donatist affair was a strange mixture of a religious issue, personal pique, and social stratification. The religious issue was a revival of the problem of how to treat those who had lapsed in persecution. Under Diocletian the specific offense was the betrayal of the Scriptures; that is, the offenders had complied with the order of the government to deliver up copies of the sacred books. Many of the bishops had felt that the saving of lives was defensible by compliance as to books. But in this instance the congregations were more intransigent than the bishops. The Donatists would have no fellowship with the *traditores*. (The word means literally "those who handed over." It is the word from which traitor is derived.) That the lapsed could be forgiven was a well established principle, but could the clergy who had betrayed the Scriptures be restored to office? And if a *traditor* had ordained another, was the ordination valid? On all of these counts, the Donatists answered in the negative.

In Carthage they received support from the disgruntled. There was a wealthy woman, by name Lucilla, described as *potens et factiosa,* who nourished a grudge against Bishop Caecilian because when a deacon he had forbidden her to bring to church and adore an unauthenticated bone of a martyr. Some of the lower clergy who had themselves aspired to the episcopate joined the dissidents. But the great strength of Donatism was to be found outside of Carthage in Numidia. All the bishops of that region took umbrage because Caecilian had been consecrated in their absence. Carthage had reason not to want them because Numidia was a land of villages and steppes, agrarian in culture, peopled by the submerged elements in the population, the Punic and the Berber. Northern Africa had been the land of the Berbers until the Punic invaders pushed them into the less fertile hill country. Then the Romans destroyed Carthage and demoted the Punic population to be merely tillers of the soil. The aristocracy in northern Africa was Latin and concentrated mainly in the cities.

Anti-Roman feeling never ceased to smolder among the submerged. The suggestion is plausible that the Ber-

bers embraced Christianity precisely because it was persecuted by the Roman government. And even Latin Africans like Tertullian, and later Augustine, were deeply
mindful of the sins of Rome against their land. Among
those disaffected toward the empire, imperial favor to the
Church was by no means an advantage. When a split occurred and the Bishop of Carthage sided with Rome in
taking a lenient attitude toward the *traditores,* Constantine
thereupon instructed his proconsul to restore church property and declared that the recipient in Africa should be
the church of the Latin aristocracy. After this development, the Punic and the Berber elements found expression
for their anti-Romanism in sectarianism. They claimed
to be the church of the pure, the church of the martyrs.
Disorderly elements began ravaging the countryside, destroying Catholic churches and throwing acid into the
eyes of the Catholic bishops. These marauding bands
were called Circumcellions. When pursued by the authorities they might resist or they might throw themselves
over cliffs in order to win the crown of the martyrs. Here
we have the first clear instance in Church history of a
coincidence of a split in the Church with a fissure in the
social structure, and this may well explain why Donatism
lasted so long. Other schisms and heresies died out;
Donatism lasted until the Mohammedan invasions and
may then have succumbed only because Islam offered a
better way of resisting Rome.

Little did Constantine realize how many factors were
involved in the controversy. When the Donatists appealed to him for judgment, he referred the case to the
Bishop of Rome who decided against them. They appealed again, asking for a court of Gallic Bishops. In A.D.
314 Constantine summoned a council of the whole of the
West to meet at Arles in Gaul. Here again the verdict
went against the Donatists. The decision was that those
who had betrayed the Scriptures might be restored to the
Church, even the clergy. Ordination if performed by a
traditor was valid if the candidate was qualified. The rite
of ordination, therefore, did not depend upon the character of the one who performed it. Baptism was declared
to be valid even if performed by a heretic. (*See Document 9, 1.*) The whole African church since the days of

Cyprian had repeated the baptism of converts from heretical sects even though Rome had condemned the practice. At Arles the African Catholics abandoned their opposition and aligned themselves with Rome. Then the Donatists conserved the earlier African view. When the Donatists refused to accept the decision at Arles, Constantine heard the case and he too decided against them. Still they would not comply. The emperor tried force but to no avail. Constantine was reduced to enjoining the Catholics to suffer in patience in the hope of reclaiming the refractory.

The Arian Controversy. Some ten years later, after the outbreak of the Donatist affair, word reached the emperor that another controversy was raging in Egypt between Bishop Alexander and Arius. This is called the Arian controversy. The dispute this time concerned doctrine rather than discipline. No social issues were involved. The Egyptian Church did not at this time split along the lines of Greek and Coptic. That came a century later. But there was a controversy, and a very lively one. Arius wrote poems about theology which were sung by dockhands and actors in the theaters. Constantine addressed a letter of remonstrance to the dissidents. "O most merciful providence of God," he wrote, "what a wound did my ears receive when I learned that the East was engaged in strife." During the schism in the West, he had looked to the East where Christianity had its rise to establish a harmony. But now!!! The emperor sent the letter by the hand of his ecclesiastical adviser, Hosius, Bishop of Cordova in Spain. But neither Hosius' diplomacy nor the emperor's admonition availed to stop the wrangling over points which the emperor stigmatized as obscure and inconsequential. Plainly, Constantine was not a theologian and had no feeling for the subtlety of the Greek intellectual tradition.

Neither Arius nor his bishop, later to be succeeded by the more famous Athanasius, would concede that the issue was trivial. Both parties took their start from divergent emphases in the theology of Origen, who asserted the eternal timeless generation of the Son of God but made the Son subordinate to the Father. The Arians, insisting on his subordination, denied the other affirmation of Origen, saying that generation must take place in time and if Christ were generated, then "there was when he was not and he was made out of nothing." (*See Document No. 9, II.*) He was indeed the first born of all creation and God's agent in the creation of all else, but he was himself created and therefore subject to change. Athanasius held that unless the Son is eternally the Son, the Father cannot be eternally the Father. And if the Son is subject to change, there is no sure ground for our salvation.

The upshot was that Constantine called a council. In the Donatist affair he had tried out three methods of dealing with disputes: one was reference to the Bishop of Rome, the second was hearing the case himself, and the third was the summoning of a council. This was the course he had come to deem preferable and he it was who summoned the first ecumenical council, that is the first general council of both the West and the East, which met at Nicaea in the year 325.

The council was attended by more than three hundred bishops. Tradition made the number 318, corresponding to the number of those circumcised in Abraham's household plus one for the Holy Spirit. Modern historians differ somewhat as to the relative roles to be ascribed to the Spirit and to the emperor. At first the attempt was made to state the faith only in Biblical terms. But the Arians would accept all Biblical language; therefore, extra-biblical terminology had to be employed in order to exclude their position. And the word chosen to represent the Church's position was *homoousios*. The Fathers had to be persuaded that the word, condemned because of its misuse by Paul of Samosata, might be properly employed. The conclusion was that the Son is of one being or essence or substance with the Father and those who say that there was a time when he was not or that he was made out of nothing or that his being is different from that of the Father are anathema.

The Spirit was included in the formulation. (*See Document No. 9, III, A.*) Thus the doctrine of the Trinity became the official teaching of the church. It is a rich doctrine which seeks to combine in a single formula the truths that God is both being and person, both static and dynamic, both one and many; that Christ is both God and Man, both beyond time and in time. No formula can state all this with precision and the doctrine of the three-in-one must not be treated as mathematics. The Arians were the logic choppers who tried to render the doctrine ridiculous by reducing it to a syllogism.

Two of the Arians at Nicaea, including Arius, would not sign the creed. Three others would not subscribe to the condemnation of persons. All five were banished by imperial decree. The penalty for refusal to deliver up the books of Arius should be death. The arm of the state, formerly used to coerce the Christians, was now employed to coerce the heretics.

But the ascendency of orthodoxy was brief. The West was Orthodox, but Asia Minor leaned toward Arianism. To Constantine Arius addressed a conciliatory and theologically ambiguous letter which satisfied the emperor's non-theological mind. He resolved to reopen the question and a council was held in Tyre in the year 335. The decision of Nicaea was reversed. Athanasius went into exile and Arius would have been reinstated had he not died the previous night.

Constantine died in 337 and was succeeded by his three sons: Constantine II in the area west of Italy; Constans in Italy and Greece; Constantius in the East. Each espoused the theological position dominant in his own area. Since the West was Nicene and the East Arian, the division of the West between two emperors weakened the Nicene forces and gave the edge to the Arian. Then Constantine II was eliminated and the balance swung to Constans of the Nicene Party. When Constans was assassinated, Constantius became sole ruler, and the world woke up to find itself Arian. Each shift was accompanied by the banishment of bishops, Athanasius for the sixth time. On one occasion the exiles included Hosius, Bishop of Cordova; Hilary, Primate of Gaul; Liberius, Bishop of Rome; and Athanasius, Bishop of Alexandria.

The victorious Arians then split into those who said that Christ was of like essence with the Father and those who said that he was of unlike essence. Athanasius perceived that like is closer to same than to unlike. His gesture of rapprochement was favorably received and

Christian opinion veered to the Nicene view. The ter-
giversations of politics impeded a speedy victory until
the year 380 when a westerner from Spain, Theodosius
the Great, became emperor. He thereupon summoned the
second ecumenical council at Constantinople in the year
381 which ratified the decisions of Nicaea and reaffirmed
the creed with but slight alteration. Thereafter, the Nicene
symbol (the term symbol signifies also a creed) remained
unchanged until the Antitrinitarianism of the age of the
Reformation.

Protests Against Imperial Christianity. The victory
of orthodoxy was a source of satisfaction to the orthodox
but in the course of the struggle they had learned that the
empire might embrace heresy and turn the arm of the
state against true believers. Protests were sharp. Liberius,
the Bishop of Rome, when summoned from his exile to
appear before the emperor and told that he must renounce
Athanasius, replied that the Church could not tolerate
condemnation without trial. The emperor rejoined, "How
large a portion of the earth are you that you take sides
alone with an impious man and disturb the peace of the
earth and all the universe?" Liberius answered, "Even
if I am alone the word of faith is not weakened for that."
A eunuch interrupted to say that the bishop had called
the emperor a Nebuchadnezzar. "By no means," replied
Liberius, turning to the emperor, "but you are acting as
rashly as he when you condemn a man you have not
tried." Old Hosius of Cordova who had been the ecclesiastical adviser of Constantine roundly remonstrated with
his son Constantius in terms reminiscent of the martyrs
when they reminded their judges that someday they would
stand before the bar of the judge of all the world. (*See
Document No. 10, I.*)

Protests from the pagan side were to be expected.
There had been no reason for it under Constantine, who
to the end adhered to the tolerance voiced at Milan. But
under his sons, the trend began which was eventually to
put paganism beyond the pale. The pagans then became
the advocates of that liberty which, when in power, they
had not accorded to the Christians. Symmachus based his
plea on the ground that no one religion possesses an exclusive claim. But each offers a valid way to truth; "We

look upon the same stars, the heaven is common to us all, the same world surrounds us; what matters by what art each of us seeks for truth? We cannot arrive by one and the same path at so great a secret."

The most renowned exponent of toleration among the waning pagans was Julian unjustly called the Apostate, for he had never been a Christian. (*See Document No. 10, II.*) Alienated by the cruelties of his cousin Constantius, and wearied by the sophistication of Arian syllogists, on his accession to the purple Julian espoused a curious blend of Hellenistic philosophy and popular paganism. He would recommend it but he would not enforce it. The Galileans, as he called the Christians, were to be persuaded by reason rather than by blows. Julian thus returned to the standpoint of the Edict of Milan.

Incidentally, Julian is of interest as the last great critic of Christianity in the pagan world. Coming one hundred and fifty years after Celsus, he was able to argue that Christians had corrupted Christianity. The process, he claimed, had begun within the New Testament writing for it was John's Gospel which made Jesus a God as the other three did not. In the succeeding centuries, Christians, he said, had departed from the primitive pattern in their veneration of the relics of the martyrs and in the exaltation of Mary as the Mother of God. The technical term was *Theotokos.* Julian renewed the charge of Celsus, though it appeared now much less plausible, that Christianity was too meek a religion to be a fit ally for an empire. Addressing the Alexandrians he asked them how their city had come to greatness. Was it through the teachings of the Galilean or rather through the prowess of Alexander the Great? At the same time Julian revealed the impact of Christianity in that as emperor he did not make himself *pontifex maximus* of paganism. That measure of the separation of church and state he had learned from the Church, and he paid Christianity a grudging tribute when he called upon his pagan priests to imitate the estimable deportment and hospitality of the Christians.

Monasticism. Of all the criticism of imperial Christianity, the most drastic was that of the monks. It was not simply the state which they renounced but society

itself. (*See Document No. 10, III.*) Celsus had told the
Christians in his day that they should either assume full
political responsibilities or else cease having families and
go to the desert. The monks did just that. Anticipations of
monasticism can be found before Constantine. But one
cannot fail to regard monasticism as a reaction to imperial
Christianity, in view of the coincidence of the cessation
of persecution through imperial favor and the flight to
the desert. When the masses entered the Church the elete
withdrew from the world.

There were many motives. One of the chief was moral
rigorism. Monasticism was related to the Puritan protests.
The first anchorite was a Novatianist. Significantly, Christian monasticism arose in Egypt at the same time that
Donatism began in northern Africa. A craving for the
life heroic was basic for both. The martyrs had been
holy athletes. The monks were successors to the martyrs.
In the age of persecution the soldiers of Christ had warred
against the persecutors by suffering, and the fight now still
went on against the demons, who were no less active because the persecutors had been overthrown. Since the
demons dwelt in the waterless places, the desert was fit
terrain for carrying on the battle. Some modern historians
have described monasticism as a loss of nerve but the
monks were no effete aristocrats. They were sinewy assail-
ants of the Prince of Darkness who subjected themselves
to the most devastating rigors.

At the same time the monks believed they had chosen
a safer way to perfection than in the midst of society.
In part undeniably they were reacting against the secularization and paganization of the church through its too
hasty success. Yet they were not fleeing so much from a
corrupt church or from bad men as from all men. "Flee
mankind" was their cry. Sins are social. They are committed against men and the safest way to be perfect is to
get away from men. The first type of monasticism was the
hermit type. Soon, however, the monks discovered that
solitude is not the cure for sin. The mind that is alone
can be assailed by delirious phantoms and the flames of
lust are not extinguished in an uncompanioned heart.

The monks in forsaking mankind had also to forsake
womankind. Sex was to be eliminated and sex became an

obsession. The monastic tales are full of the torments of indomitable desire and the devices for avoiding and overcoming temptation. The monk should not look upon a woman. The story is told that a certain monk, encountering the handmaids of God upon the way, turned aside; but an abbess said to him, "Hadst thou been a perfect monk, thou wouldst not have looked so close as to perceive that we were women." A monk having to carry his mother across a stream first wrapped his cloak about his hands lest touching her body should remind him of other women. The cowing of desire was the reason for many mortifications designed to keep the vitality of the body below the temperature of lust. When an old brother maintained that he was a stranger to sexual temptation, a younger monk doubted his veracity until the old monk explained that he had never allowed himself his fill of bread, water, or sleep, and thus had kept down the stings. Under such circumstances the monk often enough came to hate his body and the Platonic-Gnostic attitude toward the flesh insinuated itself into Christianity. Yet the monk never pronounced marriage a sin for others. Monasticism was, from the very outset, vocational. But it was the higher vocation and virginity exceeded marriage in excellence.

The extravagances of the first flush of monasticism were soon mitigated when it was discovered that solitude was not salutary unless alternated with society. The hermit type was superseded by the cenobitic, meaning the common life, that is, living in community. And though there was no return to family life, the monks did not persist in allowing only tom cats on the premises.

The great contribution of monasticism was that the monks, to quote Helen Waddell, "by the very exaggeration of their lives, stamped infinity on the imagination of the West." So that even those immersed in the world of sense are consumed with an insatiable thirst for the ineffable. And on earth monasticism gave an example of that quality of living which is a perpetual rebuke to those who by the killing of their fellows would extend or defend the borders of their states. Humility, patience, long-suffering, obedience, and peaceableness were the virtues of the monk.

The story is told of two old monks who had never had a quarrel. One of them for diversion proposed a dispute. The other said he knew not how. The first suggested that they take a tile, each would claim it and they would squabble. They did. The first said, "It is mine." The second replied, "I hope it is mine." "It is not," said the first, "it is mine." "Very well," answered the other, "if it is thine, take it." And they could not find a way to quarrel.

Monasticism which began as a flight from the world, ended as an instrument of the Church for the subduing of the world. The secession was turned into a vocation. There were stages. Jerome marked the alliance between monasticism and scholarship. He began his monastic career as a hermit but discovered that although he lived in the desert and beat his chest with rocks, still he was plagued by visions of dancing girls at Rome. As a therapeutic against such imaginings, he took up the study of Hebrew. The hard intellectual discipline which filled his mind was much more effective for him than keeping down his vitality by undernourishment. Having discovered this, he needed no longer to eschew the sight of women and was able to return even to Rome and to give instruction in Hebrew to the matrons of the aristocracy. At the same time he converted their daughters to a life of virginity and thereby so enraged the young men that, whereas once the cry at Rome had been "the Christians to the lions" now it was "the monks to the Tiber."

Jerome, accompanied by the widow Paula, went to Palestine and established at Bethlehem a monastery and a nunnery nearby where the men and the women could collaborate in a great work of scholarship, the translation of the Scriptures from the original Hebrew and Greek into a correct and more nearly classical Latin than that of the crude versions in vogue. Jerome's translation is called the Vulgate and is considered by the Catholic Church to be equally as inspired as the original. (*See Document No. 10, IV.*)

Monasticism was to become the training ground for the clergy. Of this Chrysostom is an example. At first, when invited to leave his cell and become a bishop, he declined on the grounds that the bishopric was too arduous. The bishop must administer the sacred mysteries, bringing down God from heaven, he must refute the heretics, preach to those accustomed to the thrills of the racetrack, supervise the widows and virgins, console and chide the married women, fraternize with men of the world, and keep his heart free from sin. If one faithfully discharged such a role, the reward in heaven would exceed that of a monk but the risk was greater. Monasticism appeared the safer course. But the lure of the arduous was irresistible and when the invitation to the bishopric was renewed, Chrysostom this time could not resist but became the Bishop of Antioch and later of Constantinople. Here is the transition from the cloister to the episcopal chair. Having become a bishop, he continued to live as a monk and in particular remained unmarried. In time celibacy, which at the outset was the rule only for the monk, came to be obligatory also for the priest. But this rule was not universally applied in the West until the eleventh century, and in the East to this day the lower clergy may marry.

The monastery became also a retreat for the clergy who needed some escape from the multifarious and incessant demands of the parish. Ambrose at this point affords an example. As a bishop, he had tasks to discharge which Chrysostom had not included in his list of the onerous. Before being a bishop, Ambrose had been the pretorian prefect of northern Italy, and administrator of the Roman state. He had had no thought of entering the Church. But when he came to Milan, to keep the peace during an episcopal election, the populace chose him by acclaim and ran him from baptism to the bishopric in a week. But the emperors were of no mind to lose so useful an administrator and therefore, when negotiations were necessary with invading barbarians, Ambrose was sent as ambassador. In other words, he anticipated the system in which clerics undertook offices of state.

This is not to imply that Ambrose became merely a subservient agent of the government. He is renowned for his independence. When the Empress Justina, an Arian, demanded one church in Milan for the Arians, Ambrose refused to yield the basilica which she had chosen. He ensconced himself in the building with his congregation and fortified their endurance by teaching them to sing hymns of his own composition, until the empress capitulated. And when Theodosius, the orthodox, offended in a different way by causing seven thousand at Thessalonika to be massacred as punishment for defiance of an imperial decree, Ambrose met him at the church door when he came for communion and refused him admission.

Ambrose was a very busy man, yet whenever he could steal away a day, he withdrew to a monastery.

The man who drew together all of the strands of earlier Christianity, who summed up antiquity and anticipated the Middle Ages, was Augustine. He had been a teacher of pagan rhetoric and was steeped in the classics. He had pursued a tortuous pilgrimage through the religions of his age, Manichaeanism, a more extreme variety of Gnosticism, Skepticism, Neoplatonism—he had known the experience of ecstasy in union with the ineffable One. He was a Roman imbued with Roman civic spirit, and yet he became a monk. He was an African and the wrongs of his country at the hands of Rome had seared his soul. As a Christian he had a deep understanding for the Apostle Paul's picture of man as depraved and dependent for his salvation solely on the grace of God. But for Augustine, Christianity was not simply the Gospel of redemption without regard to the deeds of men. The ethical emphasis was strong, even though he was not as rigoristic as the sects. Whereas the Church in his day had acquiesced in the wars of Rome, Augustine had a feeling for the non-resistance of the Sermon on the Mount. Yet he would not be absolutely non-resistant, and formulated the theory of constraint in religion. He would not, however, go to the length of using the penalty of death. His works supplied material for the inquisitors and for the advocates of religious liberty, for monks and for emperors, for Protestants and for Catholics.

After his conversion, he became a monk, only like Chrysostom to be co-opted for the priesthood. He became the Bishop of Hippo in northern Africa, where the Donatists had the upper hand. Because of their violence, the government, against the advice of Augustine, stepped in and used coercive measures, imprisonment and fines, to subdue them. In consequence many Donatists came over to the Catholic Church claiming to have been convinced

not by force but by the persuasive arguments to which
force had enabled them to listen by removing intimida-
tion from their own side. In the face of such testimony,
Augustine withdrew his objection to constraint and justified it by the analogy of a doctor who amputates a limb
or a horticulturalist who prunes a bough to save the
whole. Augustine did not personify the state and did not
treat the heretic as the limb to be removed by death. His
analogies were not to be taken to the letter and implied
only that the painful may be salutary. When, centuries
later, the state was regarded as the body, the heretic as
the gangrenous member, and death as amputation, the
theory of the Inquisition was complete.

The great catastrophe which confronted Augustine was
the sack of Rome in the year 411 by Alaric. The shock to
a generation which had believed in *Roma aeterna* was
incalculable. The pagans raised their voices to charge that
the cause was the abandonment of the ancient gods. Augustine set himself to face two problems: How was the
fall of Rome to be explained and what should be done
about resisting the barbarians? As for the fall of Rome,
the cause was certainly not the advent of Christianity for
Rome had been subject to calamities long before Christianity came into the world. The fall of Rome was rather
retribution for her misdeeds and Augustine, with all the
virulence of an African, chronicled the ruthlessness by
which Roman power had been extended. For him the
reign of Augustus marked no improvement, for this was
the beginning of the empire and "what are great states
without justice if not robbery on a large scale?" Rome
is said to have conferred benefits upon the conquered.
What benefits? Had they not laws and senate chambers
apart from Rome? And if there were benefits, at what
cost in blood had they been conferred? As a Britain re-
marked, "The Romans make a desert and they call it
peace." But then in Augustine's view a change did come
in the history of Rome with the conversion of Constantine. And if there were such emperors as Constantine and
Theodosius then let their sway increase. The objection to
large states was thus overcome by the reflection that
without justice they are robbery but in a state under a
Christian ruler justice is possible. The original argument

at this point appears to have been undercut, for if the fall of Rome was the punishment for the sins of pagan Rome why should the retribution have been visited upon Christian Rome? If Augustine had an answer, it appears to be that history is not after all amenable to a moralistic explanation. Nations, whether in their rise or fall, are driven by the lust of power. God suffers them to rise and casts them down at His good pleasure rather than with an eye to their desert.

But if it were God's pleasure that Rome fall, why not let her fall? Should not the Christian submit to the inscrutable will of the Almighty? Boniface, the general in charge of the defense of northern Africa against the Vandals, was so inclined. He had just lost his wife and wanted to retire and become a monk. "For God's sake not now," said Augustine. "Not everyone is privileged to be a monk; you must defend the empire." Boniface complied with the demand and married again. Augustine chided him for this but Boniface was going to have it one way or the other.

Augustine's primary point was that no matter how the empire arose, it had come to embody order and this order was not to be supinely relinquished. Then he proceeded to elaborate a Christian ethic of war. In so doing he took over from Cicero the classical code of the just war, subjecting it to certain Christian modifications. The classical code required that a just war be fought under the auspices of the state. Its intention must be to vindicate justice and restore peace. Violence should never be wanton. Noncombatants should be spared and good faith kept with the enemy. Augustine added that a just war required an unjust war. In a war only one side could be just. He was the father of the war-guilt theory. To the concern for justice and peace he added that the motive must be love. He had four categories of persons with differing codes. The magistrate alone could determine the justice of the cause and commence hostilities. The common man could use the sword only at the behest of the magistrate. In private relations he should be absolutely non-resistant. Here the Sermon on the Mount was literally conserved. The minister should be exempt because he serves at the altar and the monk should abstain because he is dedicated to the councils of perfection.

Out of the collapse of Rome from the military point of view Augustine envisaged the rise of a new society under the auspices of the Church. The eschatalogical hope of the Lord's coming was by him indefinitely postponed and the reign of the saints was not to be deferred to that consummation. The saints now begin their reign. Here is the suggestion to be implemented centuries later of a theocratic society. But such a society will not attain perfection which lies beyond the grave. (*See Document No. 11, I.*)

The Byzantine Church. In the East the trend was in quite another direction, toward what has come to be called Caesaro-papism, in which the civil ruler takes the lead in an integrated Christian society in such a way that the Caesar may be called the pope. The system was indeed integrated in what the easterners call a *symphonia*. But the society was not united. Church and state were merged but the eastern empire split along the lines of race and language accentuated by ecclesiastical divisions.

A century after the Council of Nicaea new theological controversies broke out, having now to do with the relationship of the human and the divine in Christ. The fight with the Gnostics had established that Jesus was truly a man with a real body. The Arian controversy had established that he was God, one of the three persons in the Trinity. If then he was both man and God, how could humanity and divinity be united in one person? In general, orthodoxy has been integrating, whereas the heresies have been dualistic. Gnosticism had the dualism of spirit and flesh; Arianism encompassed the dualism of creator and created and made of Christ a creature. The Christological controversies of the fifth century had to do with a dualism between the divine and the human natures in Christ.

The orthodox position in this regard rested upon a long tradition which had held that humanity and divinity do not exclude each other. The epistle of Second Peter in the New Testament speaks of believers as "partakers in the divine nature." Redemption itself for the Fathers of the Greek church consisted of becoming divine. Irenaeus said that the reason for the incarnation was that God became man in order that man might become God. In a sense the Trinitarian relationship was extended to all humanity except that a unique place was reserved for Christ. Still it was not altogether unique, for he assumed our humanity in order that we, through him, might share in his divinity.

This type of thought was challenged in two directions. The first was the position of those who tended to split Christ into a dual personality, God and man dwelling together like those who stand side by side in the same temple. This was the view ascribed to Nestorius, the bishop of Constantinople. The discovery in modern times of a theological treatise by him reveals that he was by no means as extreme as was claimed and he was ready to subscribe to the creed of the Council of Chalcedon which condemned him. His objection was to the popular deification of Jesus to the exclusion of his humanity and particularly to the expression which had offended Julian the Apostate that Mary is *Theotokos,* the Mother of God. "I cannot think of God as two or three weeks old," said Nestorius.

The bishop of Alexandria, Cyril, vigorously opposed Nestorius. Rome sided with Alexandria. Nestorius was condemned by the Council of Ephesus in 431. He died in exile. His followers formed a church in Syria which pushed into Persia and found there a readier hearing because the Persians hated the Greeks and a form of Christianity which the Greeks rejected was therefore more palatable to them. From Persia the Nestorians went into China where they left as a memorial the Nestorian stone with Chinese characters on the face and Syriac on the side. The sect disappeared in China but persists to our own day in Iran.

The other attack on the orthodox view came from the Monophysites. The word means "of one nature," the claim being that Christ had only one nature, the divine. As a matter of fact, the Monophysites were not as extreme as was claimed. Their primary concern was that no possible room be left for divergence between Christ and God. At the same time one cannot overlook Gnostic tendencies in Monophysitism, with such an emphasis on

the divine in Christ, that his human body verged on the
negligible, if not the unreal.

As in the Nestorian heresy, three sees were involved,
Constantinople, Alexandria, and Rome. In this instance,
also, after a dispute had arisen in the East, Rome cast
the deciding vote. This time the heretical view, though
starting in Constantinople, was condemned by its bishop,
Flavian, and found support rather in Alexandria. The
initiator of the heresy was a monk of Constantinople by
name Eutyches, who was willing to admit that prior to the
incarnation Christ had two natures, but thereafter, only
one. A council was called at Ephesus in 449. Such violence was used against Flavian that he died apparently
as a result. Leo I, the Bishop of Rome, dubbed this as
the "Robber Council." The next year under a new emperor, another council was called at Chalcedon (A.D. 450)
where both the Nestorian and Monophysite positions were
condemned. Rome supported the decision and the "Tome"
of Bishop Leo was the basis for the statement of faith.

The Creed of Chalcedon affirmed the full deity and the
full humanity of Christ *in* two natures. The word *in* may
have been a concession to the Monophysites because it
could be interpreted in the sense of Eutyches that Christ
only before the incarnation was *in* two natures rather than
eternally *of* two natures. But a plethora of saving adjectives guarded the orthodox meaning. (*See Document 9,
III, B*.) The creeds of Nicaea and Chalcedon rounded out
the basic theology for both the eastern and western
churches.

But Chalcedon was no more accepted by the Monophysites than by the Nestorians. Three distinct Monophysite churches arose, the Jacobite in Syria, the Abys-
sinian in Egypt, and the Armenian in Asia. Since the
Syrians, as to theology, had both Nestorian and Monophysite churches, the suspicion is obvious that the primary concern was to disagree with the Greeks. In Egypt
the Copts or Abyssinians adopted the Monophysite view
and thus Egypt was divided into Greek and Coptic elements, just as northern Africa had been divided a century
earlier by the Donatist controversy which had leagued
the Punic and the Berber elements against the Latins.

The Armenian Church, called the Gregorian, was also Monophysite.

The policy of the eastern emperors from then on was to try to win back the monophysites because their defection weakened the empire from the military point of view, and as a matter of fact later facilitated the Mohammedan invasions. The Emperor Justinian attempted conciliation by calling a council at Constantinople in the year 551. This was the fifth ecumenical council. It condemned "the three chapters," actually passages from the works of three theologians of Nestorian leanings who had not been personally condemned by the Council of Chalcedon. But this gesture did not attain its goal. The dissidents remained irreconcilable.

In the meantime, Justinian, for those areas under his control, worked out a consolidated system of law in his codification of the Roman tradition. What was later called the Roman law was the *Codex Justinianus*. It included many ecclesiastical provisions. The civil government should require the bishops to hold synods. The bishop must be unmarried. He might be a widower, provided he had been only once married. He must be over thirty, educated, and of honorable life. Legislation against heretics, pagans, and Jews was incorporated from the enactments of earlier emperors. (*See Document No. 11, II.*) Pagans were now denied the right to make sacrifices on pain of death. All Manichees were subject to the death penalty. Jews lost all civil status. Since the pagans died out and the Jews survived, they were to stand out as tolerated aliens in a Christian commonwealth. As for the heretics, the penalty of death was decreed for the repetition of baptism—this was directed against the Donatists; and against the denial of the doctrine of the Trinity—this was aimed at the Arians. These two decrees were to be revived in the sixteenth century against the Anabaptists and the Antitrinitarians.

The Eastern Church, of course, did not end with Justinian and has continued under the Turks until our own time. But the age of Justinian is the convenient point at which to terminate a sketch of the early Church.

In the West in the meantime the barbarians invaded; the government collapsed; the Church stepped in to assume many of the functions of government. The great task was to convert the barbarians to orthodox Christianity, either from paganism or from Arianism because some of the tribes were Arian before entering the empire. The process of their education and civilization also fell largely to the Church.

Three agencies were active in the endeavor. One was the papacy which initiated missionary endeavors and exercised oversight, although by no means all of the missionary movements emanated from Rome. In several instances newly won territories converted their neighbors quite independently. The second great agency was monasticism which became the militia of the papacy for the winning of the West. The third was the political power, especially the kingdom of the Franks, which supported the endeavors of the Church and enlisted churchmen extensively in the civil service.

The Church, which in the East did so much to disintegrate the empire, in the West became the builder of Christendom, which however attenuated still survives as western civilization.

PART II
DOCUMENTS AND READINGS

THE ROMAN GOVERNMENT AND THE CHRISTIANS

I. The Neronian Persecution

Tacitus, *Annals* XV, 44.

No device availed, neither public largess, nor princely munificence, nor placation of the Gods to dispel the infamous suspicion that the fire had been started at the [Emperor's] command. Therefore, to quiet the rumor, Nero cast the blame and ingeniously punished a people popularly called Christians and hated for their crimes. They took their name from Christ who had been executed in the reign of Tiberius during the procuratorship of Pontius Pilate. This noxious superstition, suppressed for the moment, broke out again not only in Judaea, where it began, but even in Rome itself, where the scum of shame flows and becomes the vogue. Therefore, those who confessed were taken and on their delation, a vast multitude was convicted not so much of arson as of hatred of the human race. To their sufferings was added mockery, for they were sewn in the skins of beasts and torn to pieces by dogs. Many died on crosses or at the stake. Others, as day declined, were burned to illumine the night. Nero gave his gardens for the spectacle and put on a circus, himself mingling with the crowd in the costume of a charioteer or driving in a chariot. Whence, though the victims were deserving of the severest penalty, nevertheless compassion arose on the ground that they suffered not for the public good but to glut the cruelty of one man.

II. The Policy of Trajan

Pliny *Epis.* X, 96 and 97. Between A.D. 111 and 113.

Pliny to the Emperor. . . . I have never been present at the trial of Christians. For that reason I do not know what or how much to punish or to ask. I have hesitated no little whether any distinction should be made for age, whether the weak should be more leniently treated than the strong, whether pardon should be granted on repentance, whether he who has been a Christian should profit by renunciation, whether profession of the name should be punished if there be no attendant crime or whether only the crimes associated with the name are subject to penalty. In the meantime I have taken the following course with those who were denounced to me as Christians. I asked them whether they were Christians. If they confessed, I asked a second and a third time with threat of penalty. If they persisted I ordered their execution, for I do not doubt that whatever it was that they profess, certainly their stubbornness and inflexible obstinacy deserved to be punished.

There were others addicted to the same madness who, because they were Roman citizens, I sent to Rome. Soon after this incident, as usually happens when the crime spreads, a variety of cases appeared. An anonymous denunciation was laid before me containing many names. Those who denied that they were Christians or had been, who in my presence supplicated and placed incense and wine before your image, which I ordered placed among the statues of the gods, especially when they cursed Christ, which those who are really Christians cannot be brought to do, these I thought should be released. Some, denounced by an informer, at first said that they were Christians and then denied it. Some said that they had been, but had ceased to be, some three years ago, some several years back and one even twenty years ago. These all worshiped your image and those of the gods and cursed Christ. They said that this was the sum of their fault or error, that they were accustomed at dawn on a stated day, to come together and sing a hymn to Christ as to a god, and that they mutually bound themselves on oath not in order to commit any crime but to refrain from theft, robbery, adultery, perjury or denial of trust funds. Then they disbanded and came together again to take food in common and quite harmless and this custom they had discontinued after my order in compliance with your mandate against forbidden societies. . . .

The Emperor Trajan to Pliny. . . . You have followed the proper procedure in dealing with the Christians who were brought before you. No absolute rule can be laid down. They are not to be hunted out. If they are denounced and convicted, they are to be punished, but he who denies that he is a Christian and proves it by supplicating our gods, although suspect in the past, may gain pardon from penitence. Anonymous accusations are not to be entertained with respect to any crime. These are the worst examples of our age.

III. Decius, A Certificate of Pagan Sacrifice, A.D. 250, "Pauni 20."

This document is No. 658, Pauni is the Egyptian month which in a normal year ran from April 26 to May 25. (Bernard P. Grenfell and Arthur S. Hunt, The Oxhyrncus Papyri, Part IV, Egyptian Exploration Fund, Graeco-Roman Branch, London: Printed by Horace Hart, 1904.)

To the superintendents of offerings and sacrifices at the city from Aurelius . . . the son of Theodorus and Pantonymis, of the said city. It has ever been my custom to make sacrifices and libations to the gods, and now also I have in your presence in accordance with the command poured libations and sacrificed and tasted the offerings together with my son Aurelius Dioscorus and my daughter Aurelia Lais. I therefore request you to certify my statement. The 1st year of the Emperor Caesar Gaius Messius Quintus Trajanus Decius Pius Felix Augustus, Pauni 20.

IV. Gallienus, The Edict of Toleration, A.D. 261

Eusebius, *Church History, PNF* ser. 2, vol. 1, p. 302.

The Emperor Caesar Publius Licinius Gallienus Pius Felix Augustus to Dionysius, Pinnas, Demetrius and the other bishops. I have ordered the bounty of my gift to be declared through the world that they [the heathen] may depart from the places of worship. And for this purpose you may use this copy of my rescript that no one may molest you. And this which you are now enabled lawfully to do, has already for a long time been conceded by me. Therefore, Aurelius Cyrenius, who is the chief administrator of affairs, will observe this ordinance which I have given.

[*Sources credited* PNF *refer to literature published in the* Post-Nicene Fathers; ANF *refers to the* Ante-Nicene Fathers. *See bibliography, page 179.*]

— Reading No. 2 —

THE MARTYRS

I. The Martyrdom of Polycarp, A.D. 155-56

All the documents in this section are taken from E. C. E. Owen, Some Authentic Acts of the Early Martyrs (London, S.P.C.K.).

✓   ✓   ✓

The excellent Polycarp, on hearing the news was not dismayed, but wished to remain in the city; but the greater number urged him to depart secretly. And so he did, to a little farm, not far from the city, and passed the time with a few companions, doing naught else but pray night and day for all and for the Churches throughout the world, as was his custom. And while praying he fell into a trance three days before he was taken, and saw his pillow being consumed by fire. And he turned and said to those with him, 'I must be burned alive.'

While his pursuers were still waiting for him, he went away to another farm, and immediately they followed close upon him. Not finding him, they laid hands on two young slaves, one of whom confessed under the torture. Now it was impossible Polycarp should escape, since his betrayers belonged to his own household. And the justice of the peace, whose lot it was to bear the same name as Herod, was in a hurry to bring him into the stadium, that he being made partner with Christ, might fulfill his lot, and his betrayers might meet the same punishment as Judas.

Taking the young slave with them, the constables and horsemen armed in the usual way went out on the Preparation about the dinner-hour 'as against a thief' at a

run. Coming up in a body late in the day they found him
lying in a cottage in an upper room; he could indeed have
escaped from thence also elsewhere, but he refused, saying, 'The will of the Lord be done.' Hearing then that
they were come he went down and talked with them,
those present marvelling at his great age and his constancy, and at their excessive eagerness to take a man so
old. So he bade food and drink to be set before them at
that hour, as much as they wanted; and besought them
to give him an hour to pray undisturbed. On leave being
given he stood and prayed, being so full of the grace of
God that for two hours he could not once be silent, and
the hearers were astonished, and many repented for having assailed an old man so godlike.

When at length he ended his prayer after remembering
all that ever had dealings with him, great and small, well-
known and unknown, and the whole Catholic Church
throughout the world, the time having now come for his
departure, they set him on an ass and brought him to
the city, it being a High Sabbath. He was met by Herodes,
the High Sheriff, and by Herodes' father, Nicetes, who,
having transferred him to the carriage, sat down beside
him, and strove to persuade him with these words: 'What
is the harm of saying, 'Caesar is Lord,' and offering incense,' with more to this effect, 'and saving your life?'
At first he made them no answer, but, when they persisted, he said: 'I do not intend to do as you advise me.'
Failing to persuade him, they reviled him, and made him
descend with so much haste that in getting down from
the carriage he hurt his shin. He, as though nothing had
happened, paid no heed, but went on quickly with much
eagerness on his way to the stadium, where the din was
so great that none could be so much as heard.

As Polycarp entered the stadium, there came a voice
from heaven, saying, 'Be strong, Polycarp, and play the
man.' None saw the speaker, but the voice was heard by
those of our brethren who were present. When he was
brought in, thereupon a great din arose as soon as they
heard 'Polycarp is taken.'

So the proconsul asked him whether he were the man.
And when he said 'Yes,' he tried to persuade him to deny
his faith, saying: 'Have respect to your age,' and other

such things as they were used to say: 'Swear by the Fortune of Caesar, repent, say "Away with the Atheists." ' Polycarp, gazing with a steadfast countenance on all the crowd of lawless heathen in the stadium, waved his hand to them, sighed, and looking up to heaven said: 'Away with the Atheists.'

When the proconsul pressed him further and said, 'Swear and I set you free: Curse Christ,' Polycarp answered, 'Eighty and six years have I served Him, and He did me no wrong. How can I blaspheme my King that saved me?'

When the proconsul persevered saying: 'Swear by the Fortune of Caesar,' Polycarp answered: 'If you vainly imagine that I shall swear by the Fortune of Caesar, as you say, and suppose that I know not what I am, hear a plain answer, "I am a Christian." If you wish to learn the Christian's reason, give me a day and listen.' The proconsul said: 'It is the people you must convince.' Polycarp answered: 'I would have counted you worthy to be reasoned with; for we have been taught to give honour as is fit, where we can without harm, to governments and powers ordained by God, but the people I do not deem worthy to hear any defence from me.'

The proconsul said: 'I have beasts and to them I will throw you, unless you repent.' 'Bring them in,' he answered, 'For repentance from the better to the worse is no change to be desired, but it is good to change from cruelty to justice.'

The other spake again to him: 'If you despise the beasts, I will have you consumed by fire, unless you repent.' 'You threaten me,' answered Polycarp, 'with the fire that burns for an hour and is speedily quenched; for you know nothing of the fire of the judgment to come and of eternal punishment which is reserved for the wicked. Why delay? Bring what you will.'

While speaking these and many other words he grew full of confidence and joy, and his face was filled with grace, so that it fell out that not only was he not troubled by the things said to him, but on the contrary the proconsul was amazed and sent his own herald to proclaim thrice in the midst of the stadium, 'Polycarp has confessed himself to be a Christian.'

Upon this proclamation of the herald the whole multitude of heathen and Jews that dwelt in Smyrna cried aloud in ungovernable fury: 'This is the teacher of Asia, the father of the Christians, the destroyer of our Gods, who teaches many not to sacrifice or worship.' So saying they shouted beseeching Philip, the Asiarch, to let loose a lion on Polycarp. However, he said it was not lawful for him to do this, as he had concluded the wild beast combat. Then they thought good to cry with one voice that Polycarp should be burnt alive. For it must needs be that the vision revealed to him on his pillow be fulfilled, when in prayer he saw it aflame, and turning to the faithful who were with him said in prophecy: 'I must be burned alive.'

This then was brought about with great speed, more quickly than words can say, the crowd gathering together forthwith from the shops and baths wood and fuel, the Jews being particularly zealous in the work, as is their custom. When the pyre was ready, he put off all his upper garments and undid his girdle, and endeavoured to take off his shoes, which he had not been used to do before because all the faithful used to contend with one another who should first touch his body. For even before his martyrdom he was treated with all honour for the goodness of his life. So he was immediately girded with the things devised for his burning; but when they were about to nail him to the stake as well, he said: 'Leave me as I am; for he that enabled me to abide the fire, will also enable me to abide at the stake unflinching without your safeguard of nails.'

So they bound him without nailing him. And he, with his hands bound behind him, like a choice ram taken from a great flock for sacrifice, an acceptable whole burnt-offering prepared for God, looked up to Heaven and said: 'Lord God Almighty, Father of Thy well-beloved and blessed Son, Jesus Christ, through whom we have received the knowledge of Thee, God of Angels and Powers and of the whole creation and of all the race of the righteous who live before Thee, I bless Thee that Thou didst deem me worthy of this day and hour, that I should take a part among the number of the martyrs in the cup of Thy Christ to the resurrection of life eternal of soul

and body in incorruption of the Holy Spirit; among whom
may I be accepted before Thee to-day a rich and acceptable sacrifice, as Thou didst fore-ordain and foreshow
and fulfil, God faithful and true. For this above all I
praise Thee, I bless Thee, I glorify Thee through the
Eternal and Heavenly High Priest Jesus Christ, Thy Well-
beloved Son, through whom to Thee with Him and the
Holy Spirit be glory now and for evermore. Amen.'

When he had offered up the Amen, and finished his
prayer, those who had charge of the fire set light to it.
And a great flame blazing forth, we to whom it was
given to behold, who were indeed preserved to tell the
story to the rest, beheld a marvel. For the fire forming a
sort of arch, like a ship's sail bellying with the wind,
made a wall about the body of the martyr, which was in
the midst, not like burning flesh, but like bread in the
baking, or like gold and silver burning in a furnace. For
we caught a most sweet perfume, like the breath of
frankincense or some other precious spice.

At last when the impious people saw that his body
could not be consumed by the fire they gave orders that a
slaughterer should go and thrust a dagger into him. This
being done there came forth [a dove and] such a gush of
blood that it put out the fire, and all the throng marvelled
that there should be so great a difference between the
unbelievers and the elect; one of whom was the most
admirable martyr, Polycarp, an apostolic and prophetic
teacher of our time, and bishop of the Catholic Church
in Smyrna. For every word that he uttered from his
mouth, was fulfilled then and shall be fulfilled hereafter.

But the Adversary, that malicious and wicked one who
is the enemy of the race of the just, seeing the greatness
of his witness, and the blamelessness of his life from the
beginning, and that he was crowned with the crown of
immortality, and had won a prize beyond gainsaying,
made it his business that we might not even recover his
body, though many were eager so to do and to touch his
sacred flesh. At any rate he suggested to Nicetas, the
father of Herodes and brother of Alce, to intreat the
proconsul not to give us his body, 'Lest,' said he, 'They
should abandon the Crucified, and begin to worship him.'
The Jews made the same suggestions with much vehe-

mence, who also watched the body, when we were about
to take it from the fire, not knowing that we can never
abandon Christ who suffered for the salvation of those
who are being saved throughout the whole world, the
sinless for sinners, nor can we worship any other. For
Him, being the Son of God, we adore, but the martyrs
we love as disciples and imitators of the Lord, and rightly
for their unsurpassable loyalty to their own King and
Master; may it be granted us to have partnership and
fellow-discipleship with them.

So the centurion, seeing the contentiousness of the
Jews, set him in the midst and burnt him according to
their custom. So we later took up his bones, being of
more value than precious stones and more esteemed than
gold, and laid them apart in a convenient place. There
the Lord will grant us to gather so far as may be and to
celebrate with great gladness and joy the birthday of his
martyrdom, in memory of those who have fought the
good fight before us and for the training and preparation
of those to come.

Such is the story of the blessed Polycarp, who with the
eleven from Philadelphia was martyred in Smyrna, and
is more particularly remembered by all, so that he is
spoken of in every place even by the Gentiles, having
been not only a famous teacher, but also an illustrious
martyr, whose martyrdom all desire to imitate, as being
after the pattern of the gospel of Christ. Having vanquished by his patience the unjust ruler, and thus received the crown of immortality he rejoices greatly with
the apostles and with all the just, and glorifies the Almighty God and Father, and praises Our Lord Jesus
Christ, the Saviour of our souls, the Pilot of our bodies,
and the Shepherd of the Catholic Church throughout the
world.

II. Justin Martyr, A.D. 165

In the time of the wicked defenders of idolatry impious
decrees were issued in town and country against the pious
Christian folk to compel them to offer libations to vain
idols. So the saints were seized and brought before the
prefect of Rome, by name Rusticus.

When they were brought before the judgement seat,

Rusticus the prefect said to Justin: 'First of all obey the gods, and make submission to the Princes.'

Justin said: 'To obey the commands of our Saviour Jesus Christ is not worthy of blame or condemnation.'

The prefect Rusticus said: 'What doctrines do you hold?'

Justin said: 'I have endeavoured to make myself acquainted with all doctrines, but I have given my assent to the true doctrines of the Christians, whether they please the holders of false beliefs or no.'

The prefect Rusticus said: 'Do those doctrines please you, miserable man?'

Justin said: 'Yes, for the belief in accordance with which I follow them is right.'

The prefect Rusticus said: 'What belief do you mean?'

Justin said: 'That which we religiously profess concerning the God of the Christians, in whom we believe, one God, existing from the beginning, Maker and Artificer of the whole creation, seen and unseen; and concerning our Lord Jesus Christ, the Son of God, who hath also been proclaimed aforetime by the prophets as about to come to the race of men for herald of salvation and for master of true disciples. And I, being but a man, regard what I say to be of little worth in comparison of His Infinite God-head, but there is a power in prophecy, and that I acknowledge; therein hath proclamation been made aforetime of Him of whom I just spoke as the Son of God. For I know that from the beginning the prophets foretold His coming among men.'

The prefect Rusticus said: 'Where do ye meet together?'

Justin said: 'Where each wills and can. Do you really think that we all meet in the same place? Not so: for the God of the Christians is not confined by place, but being unseen fills heaven and earth, and is worshipped and glorified by the faithful everywhere.'

The prefect Rusticus said: 'Tell me, where do ye meet, or in what place do you gather your disciples?'

Justin said: 'I lodge above in the house of Martin, near the baths of Timothy, and during all this time (this is my second visit to Rome) I have known no other place of meeting but his house. And if any wished to come to me, I imparted to him the word of truth.'

Rusticus said: 'To come to the point then, are you a Christian?'

Justin said: 'Yes, I am a Christian.'

The prefect Rusticus said to Chariton: 'Tell me further, Chariton, are you also a Christian?'

Chariton said: 'I am a Christian by God's command.'

The prefect Rusticus said to Charito: 'What do you say, Charito?'

Charito said: 'I am a Christian by God's gift.'

Rusticus said to Euelpistus: 'And what are you?'

Euelpistus, a slave of Caesar, answered: 'I also am a Christian, freed by Christ, and share by the grace of Christ in the same hope.'

The prefect Rusticus said to Hierax: 'Are you also a Christian?'

Hierax said: 'Yes, I am a Christian, for I worship and adore the same God.'

The prefect Rusticus said: 'Did Justin make you Christians?'

Hierax said: 'I was, and shall ever be, a Christian.'

A man called Paeon stood up and said: 'I also am a Christian.'

The prefect Rusticus said: 'Who taught you?'

Paeon said: 'I received from my parents this good confession.'

Euelpistus said: 'I listened indeed gladly to the words of Justin, but I too received Christianity from my parents.'

The prefect Rusticus said: 'Where are your parents?'

Euelpistus said: 'In Cappadocia.'

Rusticus said to Hierax: 'Where are your parents?' He answered, saying: 'Our true father is Christ, and our mother our faith in Him. My earthly parents are dead, and I was dragged away from Iconium in Phrygia before coming hither.'

The prefect Rusticus said to Liberian: 'And what do you say? Are you a Christian? Are you an unbeliever like the rest?'

Liberian said: 'I also am a Christian; for I am a believer and adore the only true God.'

The prefect said to Justin: 'Listen, you that are said to be a learned man, and think that you are acquainted with true doctrine, if you shall be scourged and beheaded, are you persuaded that you will ascend to heaven?'

Justin said: 'I hope if I endure these things to have His gifts. For I know that for all who so live there abides until the consummation of the whole world the free gift of God.'

The prefect Rusticus said: 'Do you then think that you will ascend to heaven, to receive certain rewards?'

Justin said: 'I do not think, I know and am fully persuaded.'

The prefect Rusticus said: 'Let us now come to the pressing matter in hand. Agree together and sacrifice with one accord to the gods.'

Justin said: 'No one who is rightly minded turns from true belief to false.'

The prefect Rusticus said: 'If ye do not obey, ye shall be punished without mercy.'

Justin said: 'If we are punished for the sake of our Lord Jesus Christ we hope to be saved, for this shall be our salvation and confidence before the more terrible judgment-seat of our Lord and Saviour which shall judge the whole world.' So also said the other martyrs: 'Do what you will. For we are Christians and offer no sacrifice to idols.'

Rusticus the prefect gave sentence: 'Let those who will not sacrifice to the gods and yield to the command of the Emperor be scourged and led away to be beheaded in accordance with the laws.'

The holy martyrs went out glorifying God to the customary place and were beheaded, and fulfilled their testimony by the confession of their Saviour. And some of the faithful took their bodies by stealth and laid them in a convenient place, the grace of our Lord Jesus Christ working with them, to whom be glory for ever and ever. Amen.

III. The Letter of the Churches of Vienne and Lyons, A.D. 177

The servants of Christ dwelling in Vienne and Lyons to the brethren in Asia and Phrygia who have the same faith as we in redemption and the same hope, peace and

grace and glory from God the Father and our Lord
Christ Jesus. . . . The greatness of the tribulation here,
and the exceeding wrath of the heathen against the
Saints, and all that the blessed martyrs suffered, neither
are we capable of describing accurately, nor can it be
compassed in writing.

For the Adversary fell upon us with all his strength,
making already a prelude to his coming in full force
hereafter, and went to all lengths, practising and training
his own against the servants of God, so that not only
were we banished from houses and baths and market-
places, but it was forbidden for any of us to be seen at
all in any place whatsoever. But the grace of God took
the field against him, and protected the weak, and ranged
on the other side steadfast pillars able through their endurance to draw on themselves all the onset of the Evil
one; who also closed with him, bearing all kind of reproach and torment; who also, counting great things as
small, made haste toward Christ, showing in very truth
that 'the sufferings of this present time are not worthy to
be compared with the glory that shall be revealed in
us. . . .'

And in the first place they endured nobly what the
crowd in general heaped upon them, taunts, blows, hal-
ings, robberies, stone-throwings, beleaguerings, and all
else that a furious multitude inflicts on private and public
enemies. And then they were brought into the market-
place by the tribune of the soldiers and the magistrates
of the city, and after being examined in the presence of
the whole multitude and making their confession were
shut up in prison until the arrival of the governor. Afterwards they were brought before the governor, and he was
showing all the usual cruelty towards us. Now among the
brethren was Vettius Epagathus, one filled with the fullness of love towards God and his neighbour, whose conversation had been so rightly ordered that though young
he did not fall below the witness borne to old Zacharias,
he had indeed 'walked in all the commandments and
ordinances of the Lord blameless,' and untiring in all
service towards his neighbour, having great zeal for God
and 'fervent in the spirit.' He being of this sort did not
suffer the judgment so unreasonably being passed against

us, but was indignant on our behalf, and claimed to be heard himself, pleading in defence of the brethren that there was nothing godless or impious about us. When those about the tribunal shouted him down (for he was a man of mark), and the governor did not allow the just claim he put forward but asked no more than this, whether he too were a Christian, he confessed in a loud voice and was added to the company of the martyrs. And he was styled the advocate of the Christians, having indeed the Advocate in himself, even the Spirit of Zacharias, which he sowed through the fullness of his love, being well-pleased even to lay down his own life for the defence of the brethren. For he was and is a true disciple of Christ, 'following the Lamb whithersoever He goeth.'

After this the rest were divided: some were proto-martyrs manifest and ready, who with all zeal fulfilled their confession even unto martyrdom; then too were manifested the unready, untrained, and still feeble, unable to bear the strain of a great contest. Of these about ten in number miscarried, who also wrought in us great sorrow and grief immeasurable, and checked the zeal of those that had not yet been taken, but, in spite of all sorts of dreadful sufferings, nevertheless accompanied the martyrs and refused to leave them. Then we were all greatly distraught from uncertainty about the confession, not from fear of the torments that were coming upon us, but from looking to the end and dreading lest some should fall away. There were taken however day by day those who were worthy, and these filled up their number, so that there were gathered from the two Churches all persons of merit by whom more particularly affairs had been ordered here. There were taken, too, certain pagan slaves of ours, since the governor had given public orders for all of us to be sought out. These by the lying in wait of Satan, in fear of the tortures which they saw the Saints suffering, and urged thereto by the soldiers, falsely charged us with Thyestean banquets and Oedipodean unions and with other crimes which we are not permitted to mention or imagine, nor even to believe that such things ever happened among men.

On the spread of these reports all were like wild beasts against us, so that some who had formerly behaved with moderation out of friendship were then greatly enraged and gnashed their teeth at us. Then was fulfilled what was spoken by our Lord that there should come a time when 'whosoever killeth you will think that he doeth God service.'

After this the holy martyrs endured tortures beyond all telling, Satan being desirous that some blasphemous word should escape their lips also. Beyond measure all the fury of crowd and governor and soldiers fell on Sanctus, the deacon from Vienne, and on Maturus, newly baptized, but a noble combatant, and on Attalus, a native of Pergamus, who had always been 'a pillar and stay' of the people here, and on Blandina, through whom Christ made manifest that what things appear paltry and uncomely and contemptible are accounted of great honour with God, for their love to Him, which does not glory in appearance but is shown in power.

For when we were all in fear, and her mistress according to the flesh, herself a combatant among the martyrs, was in agony lest Blandina should not be able from weakness of body even to make her confession boldly, she was filled with so much power that even those who tortured her in relays in every way from morning until evening were faint and weary. Indeed they themselves confessed that they were beaten, having no longer any more that they might do to her, wondering that she remained alive, all her body being broken and torn, testifying that one kind of torture, let alone so many and so grievous, was enough to release her soul. But the blessed woman, as a noble athlete, renewed her strength in her confession, and it was refreshment and peace and freedom from pain amid her sufferings to repeat, 'I am a Christian, and there is no evil done among us.'

And Sanctus too endured nobly beyond all measure and all human patience all outrages at the hands of men, and, when the wicked hoped that because of the continuance and severity of the tortures something unseemly would be heard from him, with such constancy did he range himself against them that he uttered not his own name nor the name of the nation or city whence he came, nor whether he were bond or free; but to all questions answered in the Latin tongue, 'I am a Christian.' This he confessed repeatedly to serve for name and city and race and everything, and the heathen heard from him no other word.

Whence there arose great rivalry in the governor and the tormentors against him, so that when they had nothing more that they could do to him at the last they applied red-hot brazen plates to the most tender parts of his body. And these indeed were burned, but he himself continued unbent and unyielding, stout in his confession, bedewed and strengthened by the heavenly fountain of the water of life issuing from the belly of the Christ. His poor body was witness to his sufferings, for it was nothing but wound and weal, bent double, and robbed of the outward form of humanity, his body wherein Christ suffered and wrought great wonders, destroying the Adversary, and showing as a pattern to the rest that there is nothing terrible where is the love of the Father, nothing painful where the glory of Christ. For when the wicked some days later tortured the martyr again and thought that his body being swollen and inflamed, if they applied the same torments they would overcome him, since he could not bear a touch of the hand, or that by dying under torture he would frighten the rest, nothing of the sort happened in his case. Nay more, beyond all human imagining his poor body revived and was restored in the later trial, and recovered its former appearance and the use of the limbs, so that the second torture became to him through the grace of Christ not a torment but a cure.

Moreover, there was a certain Biblias, one of those who had denied the faith, and the devil, who thought that he had already devoured her, wishing to damn her by blasphemy as well, brought her to torture, that he might force her to say impious things about us, being to start with frail and timid.

But she, while she was being tortured returned to her sober mind and woke as it were from a deep slumber, being reminded by her temporal punishment of the eternal torment in hell, and directly contradicted the blasphemers, saying: 'How can those eat children, who are forbidden to eat the blood even of brute beasts?' And from this moment she confessed herself a Christian and was added to the company of the martyrs.

When the tyrants' cruelties were made of none effect by Christ through the patience of the martyrs, the devil set about contriving other devices, shutting them up in darkness in the foulest part of the prison, stretching their feet, strained to the fifth hole, in the stocks; with the other outrages which attendants angry, and full of the devil besides, are wont to inflict on prisoners; so that most of them were suffocated in the prison, as many as the Lord, manifesting forth His glory, wished so to pass away. For some, after being so cruelly tormented, that it did not seem as if they could live any longer even if every attention were given them, lingered on in prison, destitute of all human care, but confirmed by the Lord, and strengthened in body and soul, encouraging and consoling the rest. Others, young and lately taken, whose bodies had not been already inured to torture, were unable to bear the burden of confinement and died there.

Blessed Pothinus, who had been entrusted with the charge of the bishopric in Lyons, being over ninety years of age and very sick in body, scarcely breathing from the sickness aforesaid, but strengthened by zeal of the spirit from his vehement desire for martyrdom, was dragged with the others on to the tribunal, his body fainting with old age and disease, but his soul sustained within him, that thereby Christ might triumph. He was conveyed by the soldiers on to the tribunal, accompanied by the magistrates of the city and the whole multitude who cried this and that; accusing him of being also one of Christ's followers, and he 'witnessed a good confession.' Being questioned by the governor who was the God of the Christians, he answered: 'If you are worthy, you shall know.' After this he was hustled without mercy, and suffered hurts of all kinds: for those who were close showed him all manner of insolence with hand and foot, not reverencing his years, and those at a distance hurled at him anything each might have ready, all deeming that any one was guilty of great offence and impiety, who was behindhand in brutality towards him; for they thought in this way to avenge their gods. So he was cast scarcely breathing into the prison, and after two days expired.

And here took place a great dispensation of God, and there was manifested the immeasurable mercy of Christ,

after a fashion rarely known among the brotherhood, but
worthy of Christ's devising. For those who when first
taken denied the faith were imprisoned like the rest and
shared their sufferings; for their denial was of no profit
to them at all at that time, since those who confessed
to be what indeed they were, were imprisoned as Christians, having no other charge brought against them, while
the others were detained as murderers and villains, being
punished twice as hardly as the rest. For those were
comforted by the joy of their martyrdom, and the hope
of the promises, and by love towards Christ, and the
Spirit of the Father, whereas these were greatly tormented
by their conscience, so that, as they passed, they were
easily distinguished by their looks from all the rest. For
those advanced full of joy, having in their looks a mingling of majesty and great beauty, so that even their
chains were worn by them as a comely ornament, as for
a bride adorned with fringed raiment of gold richly
wrought, exhaling at the same time the 'sweet savour of
Christ,' so that some thought they had been anointed with
perfume of this world, but these downcast, dejected, ill-
favoured, full of all unseemliness, taunted beside by the
heathen as base and cowardly, bearing the reproach of
murderers, but having lost their universally honourable
and glorious and life-giving name. The rest seeing this
were strengthened, and those who were taken afterwards
made their confession undoubtingly, giving not so much
as a thought to the devil's arguments.

[*After some further remarks they continue.*] After this
their martyrdoms were parcelled into deaths of all sorts.
For plaiting one crown of different colours and all kinds
of flowers they offered it to the Father; it was needful
indeed that the noble athletes should endure a manifold
conflict and win a great victory before they received the
great crown of immortality.

Maturus, then, and Santus and Blandina and Attalus
were taken into the amphitheatre to the beasts to give
the heathen a public spectacle of cruelty, a special day
being appointed because of our brothers for a fight with
beasts. And Maturus and Sanctus again went in the
amphitheatre through every form of torture, as though
they had suffered nothing at all before; or rather, as hav-

ing overcome the adversary already in many bouts, and contending now for the final crown of victory, they bore the usual running of the gauntlet of whips, and the mauling by the beasts, and everything else that the maddened people, on this side or on that, clamoured for and demanded, and on the top of all the iron chair, whereon their bodies were roasted and filled with the savour the nostrils of the people. But they did not rest even so, but were more mad than ever, in their desire to overcome the martyrs' endurance, yet not even then did they hear from Sanctus aught else save the word of his confession he had been wont to utter from the beginning. These, then, after their spirits had long held out through a great contest, when in place of all the diversity of single combats they had been throughout that day a spectacle to the world, were offered up at last. But Blandina was exposed hung on a stake to be the food of the beasts let loose on her. Alike by the sight of her hanging in the form of a cross and by her earnest prayer she put much heart in the combatants; for they saw during the contest even with the eyes of flesh in the person of their sister Him who was crucified for them, to assure those who believed on Him that every one who suffereth for the glory of Christ hath for ever fellowship with the living God. And as none of the beasts at that time touched her, she was taken down from the stake and brought back again to the prison, to await another contest, that having won in many trials she might make that 'crooked Serpent's' condemnation irreversible, and inspire her brethren—she, the little, the weak, the contemptible—who had put on Christ, the great and invincible athlete, and had worsted in many bouts the adversary, and through conflict crowned herself with the crown of immortality.

Attalus, too, being loudly called for by the crowd (for he was a man of repute), entered the arena as a combatant well-prepared by his good conscience, for he was soundly trained in the Christian discipline, and had ever been a witness to truth amongst us. He was being led around the amphitheatre with a placard preceding him, on which was written in Latin: 'This is Attalus the Christian,' the people being violently inflamed against him, when the governor learning that he was a Roman citizen ordered him to be remanded with the rest that were in the prison, and, having written a dispatch to Caesar concerning them, waited his sentence.

The interval was not idle nor unfruitful to them, but through their patience was made manifest the immeasurable mercy of Christ. For the dead were made alive through the living, and martyrs showed kindness to those who were not martyrs, and there was much joy in the heart of the Virgin Mother, in recovering alive those untimely births she had cast forth as dead. For through them the most part of those who had denied the faith entered again into their mother's womb, and were conceived again, and quickened again, and learned to make their confession, and alive already and braced came to the tribunal (for He who hath no pleasure in the death of the wicked made sweet their bitterness, and God was gracious to them unto repentance), that they might again be questioned by the governor. For the command of Caesar was that these should be beheaded, but that those who denied the faith should be set free. So as it was the beginning of the festival here (it is thronged by an assemblage of all peoples), the governor brought the blessed ones to the tribunal, making a gazing-stock and a show of them to the multitude. Therefore he examined them again, and beheaded those who appeared to possess Roman citizenship, and sent the rest to the beasts.

And Christ was greatly glorified in those who had formerly denied the faith, but then contrary to the expectation of the heathen made their confession. For they were privately examined with the intent they should be set free, and confessing were added to the company of the martyrs. There remained outside those who had never had even a vestige of the faith, nor any knowledge of the wedding garment, nor any thought of the fear of God, but through their conversation blasphemed the Way, that is the sons of perdition.

All the rest were added to the Church. As they were being examined, a certain Alexander, Phrygian by birth, doctor by profession, who had spent many years in the Gauls, and was known to almost all for his love to God and his boldness in preaching the Word (for he was not without a share in the Apostolic gift), was standing by the tribunal and urging them by signs to confession, and so became manifest to those surrounding the tribunal as one in travail. The multitude, angered at the renewed confession of those who had formerly denied the faith, clamoured against Alexander as the cause of this. So when the governor had ordered him to be set before him, and asked him who he was, Alexander said: 'A Christian.' The governor in anger condemned him to the beasts, and on the next day he entered the arena with Attalus. For to gratify the people the governor had given Attalus also to the beasts, for the second time. And when they had gone through all the instruments devised for torture in the amphitheatre, and had endured a contest very great, they also were offered up at last. Alexander, indeed, neither groaned nor uttered any sound at all, but communed in his heart with God. But Attalus, when he had been placed in the iron chair, and was burning everywhere, as the savour from his body was rising upward, said to the multitude in the Latin tongue: 'Lo! as for eating of men, this is what you yourselves do; but we neither eat men nor work any other wickedness.' And being asked what was the name of God, he answered: 'God hath no name as man hath.'

After all these, on the last day of the single combats, Blandina was again brought in with Ponticus, a boy of about fifteen. They had also been led in daily to look upon the torture of the rest, and their enemies would fain have forced them to swear by their idols; but because they continued steadfast and made nought of them, the multitude was enraged against them, so that they neither pitied the age of the boy, nor reverenced the sex of the woman. They exposed them to every terror, they made them pass through every torment in turn, again and again constraining them to swear, but unable to achieve their purpose. For Ponticus, encouraged by his sister, so that even the heathen saw that she was exhorting and strengthening him, after nobly enduring every torment gave up the ghost.

The blessed Blandina last of all, like a noble mother that has encouraged her children and sent them before her crowned with victory to the King, retracing herself also all her children's battles hastened towards them, rejoicing and triumphing in her departure, as though she were called to a marriage supper, instead of being cast to the beasts. After the whips, after the beasts, after the frying-pan, she was thrown at last into a net, and cast before a bull. And after being tossed for some long time by the beasts, having no further sense of what was happening because of her hope and hold on the things she had believed, and because of her communing with Christ, she was herself also offered up, the very heathen confessing that they had never known a woman endure so many and so great sufferings.

But not even so were their madness and savagery towards the Saints appeased. For wild and barbarous peoples stirred up by that wild Beast were hard to satisfy, and their cruelty found another and peculiar outlet upon the bodies of the dead. For because they lacked human reason their defeat did not shame them, rather it fired their beast-like fury, both governor and people showing towards us the same undeserved hatred, that the Scripture might be fulfilled: 'He that is wicked, let him do wickedly still, and he that is righteous let him do righteousness still.' For those that were suffocated in the prison they threw to the dogs, watching carefully by night and day, lest we should give any of them burial. After that they exposed what the beasts and the fire had left, part torn, part charred, and the heads of the rest with the trunks; these likewise they left unburied, and watched them for many days with a guard of soldiers. Some raged and gnashed their teeth at the dead, seeking to take some more exquisite revenge upon them. Others laughed and mocked, magnifying at the same time their idols, and attributing to them the punishment of the martyrs. Others again who were more reasonable and seemed to have some degree of feeling for us, reproached us, repeating: 'Where is their God, and how did their religion which they preferred even to their lives profit them?' On their side such were the varieties of behaviour; on ours there was great sorrow because we could not bestow the bodies in the earth. For night did not help us towards this, nor money persuade, nor prayer shame, but they watched every way, as though they would derive some great profit from the martyrs' loss of burial. [*Then after some further remarks they go on.*] So the bodies of the martyrs, after being subjected to all kinds of contumely and exposed for six days, were then burnt and reduced to ashes by the impious, and swept into the river Rhone which flows hard by, that not a fragment of them might be left on earth. And they planned this, as though they could get the better of God, and rob them of the other Life; that, in their own words, 'They may have no hope of resurrection, trusting in which they introduce among us a strange and new religion, and despise tortures, going readily and with joy to death. Let us see now whether they will rise again, and whether their God can help them and deliver them from our hands.' . . .

THE LITERARY ATTACK
AND THE APOLOGIES

I. The Attack: Celsus

Excerpts from The True Word *of Celsus, A.D. 177-80 from the translation by Henry Chadwick in* Origen: Contra Celsum *(Cambridge: University Press, 1953). The references in the text are to the work of Origen.*

✓   ✓   ✓

OBSCURANTISM OF THE CHRISTIANS: [*Celsus says that*] some [*Christians*] do not even want to give or to receive a reason for what they believe, and use such expressions as 'Do not ask questions; just believe,' and 'Thy faith will save thee.' (1:9.) . . . Their injunctions are like this. 'Let no one educated, no one wise, no one sensible draw near. For these abilities are thought by us to be evil. But as for anyone ignorant, anyone stupid, anyone uneducated, anyone who is a child, let him come boldly.' By the fact that they themselves admit that these people are worthy of their God, they show that they want and are able to convince only the foolish, dishonorable and stupid, and only slaves, women and little children. (III:44.) . . . In private houses also we see wool-workers, cobblers, laundry-workers, and the most illiterate and bucolic yokels, who would not dare to say anything at all in front of their elders and more intelligent masters. But whenever they get hold of children in private and some stupid women with them, they let out some astounding statements as, for example, that they must not pay any attention to their father and school-teachers, but must obey them; they say that these talk nonsense and have no understanding, and that in reality they neither know nor are able to do anything good, but are taken up with mere empty chatter. But they alone, they say, know the right way to live, and if the children would believe them, they would become happy and make their home happy as well. And if, just as they are speaking, they see one of the school-teachers coming, or some intelligent person, or even the father himself, the more cautious of them flee in all directions; but the more reckless urge the children on to rebel. (III:55.)

THE FOOLISHNESS OF THE INCARNATION. The assertion made both by some of the Christians and by the Jews, the former saying that some God or son of God has come down to earth as judge of mankind, the latter saying he will come, is most shameful. . . . What is the purpose of such a descent on the part of God? . . . Was it in order to learn what was going on among men? . . . Does not He know everything? . . . If, then, He does know, why does He not correct men, and why can He not do this by His divine power? . . . Was He then unable to correct men merely by divine power, without sending some one specially endowed for the purpose? . . . God does not need to be known for His own sake, but He wants to give us knowledge of Himself for our salvation, in order that those who accept it may become good and be saved, but that those who do not accept it may be proved to be wicked and punished. . . . Is it only now after such a long age that God has remembered to judge the life of men? Did He not care before? . . . Either God really does change, as they say, into a mortal body; and it has already been said that this is an impossibility. Or He does not change, but makes those who see Him think that He does so, and leads them astray and tells lies. . . . The Jews say that as life is filled with all manner of evil it is necessary for God to send someone down that the wicked may be punished and everything purified, as it was when the first flood occurred. . . . Christians also add certain doctrines to those maintained by the Jews, and assert that the Son of God has already come on account of the sins of the Jews, and that because the Jews punished Jesus and gave him gall to drink they drew down upon themselves the bitter anger of God. . . . The race of Jews and Christians [*are compared by Celsus*] to a cluster of bats or ants coming out of a nest, or frogs holding council round a marsh, or worms assembling in some filthy corner, disagreeing with one another about which of them are the worst sinners. They say: 'God shows and proclaims everything to us beforehand, and He has even deserted the whole world and the motion of the heavens, and disregarded the vast earth to give attention to us alone; and He sends messengers to us alone and never stops sending them and seeking that we may be with Him for ever.' . . . [*Christians say*] 'Since some among us are in error, God will come or will send His Son to consume the unrighteous, and that the rest of us may have eternal life with Him.' . . . These assertions would be more tolerable coming from worms and frogs than from Jews and Christians disagreeing with one another. . . . (IV:2-30.) It is foolish of them also to suppose that, when God applies the fire (like a cook!), all the rest of mankind will be thoroughly roasted and they alone will survive, not merely those who are alive at the time but those also long dead who will rise up from the earth possessing the same bodies as before. This is simply the hope of worms. . . . (V:14.)

THE LIFE OF JESUS: Celsus quotes a Jew who says that Jesus fabricated the story of his birth from a virgin. . . . He came from a Jewish village and from a poor country woman who earned her living by spinning. . . . She was turned out by the carpenter who was betrothed to her, as she had been convicted of adultery and had a child by a certain soldier named Panthera. . . . While she was wandering about in a disgraceful way she secretly gave birth to Jesus. . . . Because he was poor he hired himself out as a workman in Egypt, and there tried his hand at certain magical powers on which the Egyptians pride themselves; he returned full of conceit because of these powers, and on account of them gave himself the title of God . . . (I:28-32). . . . Jesus collected round him ten or eleven infamous men, the most wicked tax-collectors and sailors, and with these fled hither and thither, collecting a means of livelihood in a disgraceful and importunate way. . . . (L:62.) . . . The body of a god would not have been born as you, Jesus, were born. . . . The body of a god would also not eat food. . . . (L:69-70.) . . . The Jew says: How could we regard him as God when in other matters, as people perceived, he did not manifest anything which he professed to do, and when we had convicted him, condemned him and decided that he should be punished, was caught hiding himself and escaping most disgracefully, and indeed was betrayed by those whom he called his disciples? . . . No good general who led many thousands was ever betrayed, nor was any wicked robber-chieftain. . . . But he, who was betrayed by those under his authority, neither ruled like a good general; nor when he had deceived his disciples, did he even inspire in the men so deceived that goodwill, if I may call it that, which robbers feel towards their chieftain. . . . [*The Jew*] accuses the disciples of having invented the statement that Jesus foreknew and foretold all that happened to him. . . . If he foretold both the one who was to betray him and the one who was to deny him, why did they not fear him as God, so that the one did not betray him nor the other deny him? . . . If these things had been decreed for him and if he was punished in obedience to his Father, it is obvious that since he was a god and acted intentionally, what was done of deliberate purpose was neither painful nor grievous to him. . . . Why then does he utter loud laments and wailings, and pray that he may avoid the fear of death, saying something like this, 'O Father, if this cup could pass by me'? . . . When he was alive he won over only ten sailors and tax-collectors of the most abominable character, and not even all of these. . . . Is it not utterly ludicrous that when he was alive himself he convinced nobody, but now he is dead, those who wish to do so convince multitudes? . . . While he was alive he did not help himself, but after death he rose again and showed the marks of his punishment and how his hands had been pierced. But who saw this? An hysterical female, as you say, and perhaps some other one of those who were deluded by the same sorcery. . . . If Jesus really wanted to show forth divine power, he ought to have appeared to the very men who treated him despitefully, and to the men who condemned him and to everyone everywhere. (Book II.)

POLITICAL ALOOFNESS: Reason demands one of two alternatives. If they refuse to worship in the proper way the lords in charge of the following activities, then they ought neither to come to the estate of a free man, nor to marry a wife, nor to beget children, nor to do anything else in life. But they should depart from this world leaving no descendants at all behind them. . . . But if they are going to marry wives, and beget children, and taste of the fruits, and partake of the joys of this life . . . then they ought to render due honours to the beings who have been entrusted with these things. . . . (VIII:55.) We ought not to disbelieve the ancient man who long ago declared 'Let there be one king.' . . . For, if you overthrow this doctrine, it is probable the emperor will punish you. If anyone were to do the same as you, there would be nothing to prevent him from being abandoned, alone and deserted, while earthly things would come into the power of the most lawless and savage barbarians. . . . You will surely not say that if the Romans were convinced by you and were to neglect their customary honours to both gods and men and were to call upon your Most High, or whatever name you prefer, He would come down and fight on their side, and they would have no need for any other defence. In earlier times also the same God made these promises and some far greater than these, so you say, to those who pay regard to him. But see how much help he has been to both them and you. Instead of being masters of the whole world, they [*the Jews*] have been left with no land and home of any kind. While in your case, if anyone does still wander about in secret, yet he is sought out and condemned to death. (VIII:69.)

II. The Apologists

The following excerpts from the "Apologies" are arranged under the rubrics of the main charges against the Christians.

✓   ✓   ✓

OBSCURANTISM. *The reply of Athenagoras in* A Plea for
the Christians:

Who of those that reduce syllogisms, and clear up
ambiguities, and explain etymologies, or of those who
teach homonyms and synonyms, and predicaments and
axioms, and what is the subject and what the predicate,
and who promise their disciples by these and such like
instructions to make them happy: who of them have so
purged their souls as, instead of hating enemies to love
them; and instead of speaking ill of those who have reviled them . . . to bless them? . . . But among us you
will find uneducated persons, and artisans, and old women,
who, if they are unable in words to prove the benefit of
our doctrine, yet by their deeds exhibit the benefit arising
from their persuasion of its truth: they do not rehearse
speeches, but exhibit good works; when struck, they do not
strike again; when robbed they do not go to law; they
give to those that ask of them, and love their neighbors
as themselves. (Chapter XII, *ANF* II, 132.)

The reply of Origen in his Against Celsus:

[*Celsus*] criticizes *the teacher* also for seeking the stupid. We would say to him, Whom do you call stupid?
Strictly speaking, every bad man is stupid. . . . But if
by 'stupid' you mean those who are not clever but very
superstitious, I answer you that I do all in my power to
improve even these. I seek rather the cleverer and sharper
minds because they are able to understand the explanation of problems and of the hidden truths set forth in the
law, the prophets, and the gospels. You despised these
as if they contained nothing of importance; but you did
not examine their meaning, or attempt to enter into the
purpose of the writers. (*ANF* III, 74.)

DECEPTION: *Origen replied that the disciples would not
have died for a lie and their very writing proves their
candor:*

I think that a man who examines the facts with an
open mind would say that these men would not have

given themselves up to a precarious existence for the
sake of Jesus' teaching unless they had some deep convic-
tion which he implanted in them that they should not
only live according to his precepts but should also influence others—and should do so in spite of the fact that
destruction, as far as human life is concerned, clearly
awaited anyone who ventured to introduce new opin-
ions. . . . (*ANF* I, 31.) But I think that the clear and
certain proof [*of the resurrection*] is the argument from
the behaviour of the disciples, who devoted themselves
to a teaching which involved risking their lives. If they
had invented the story that Jesus had risen from the dead,
they would not have taught with such spirit, in addition
to the fact that in accordance with this they not only
prepared others to despise death but above all despised
it themselves (*ANF* II, 57.) . . . Celsus says: As the
disciples of Jesus were unable to conceal the self-evident
fact, they conceived this idea of saying that he foreknew
everything. He [*Celsus*] did not pay attention, nor did he
want to pay attention, to the honest intentions of the
writers, who affirmed both that Jesus predicted to his
disciples, 'All of you shall be offended this night,' and
that this proved to be correct when they were offended,
and that he also prophesied to Peter, 'Before the cock
crow thou shalt deny me thrice,' and that Peter denied
three times. If they were not honest, but, as Celsus thinks,
were composing fictitious stories, they would not have
recorded Peter's denial or that Jesus' disciples were offended. (*ANF* II, 15 translation by Chadwick.*)

IMMORALITY: *Tertullian in* The Apology *in denying that
Christians were guilty of infanticide pointed out that the
pagans who brought the charge were guilty of abortion
and the exposure of children:*
   We are called the worst of criminals from the sacrament of infanticide and our feeding thereon and from
the incestuous intercourse that follows the banquets. . . .
[*How could such information come to light?*] We are
daily beseiged, we are daily betrayed, we are raided over
and over again in our very meeting places and assemblies.
Yet who ever under such circumstances came upon an

infant wailing? . . . If we are always in hiding, when was the crime that we commit betrayed? Or, rather, by whom could it be betrayed? In any case not by the accused themselves. . . . And . . . where do outsiders obtain their knowledge, since even religious initiations always exclude the profane and take precautions against the presence of spectators? . . .

As regards infanticide . . . although child-murder differs from homicide, it makes no difference whether it is done willingly or as part of a sacred rite. I will turn to you now as a nation. How many of the crowd standing round us, open-mouthed for Christian blood, how many of you gentlemen, magistrates most just and strict against us, shall I not prick in your inner consciousness as being the slayers of your own offspring? There is, indeed, a difference in the manner of the death; but assuredly it is more cruel to drown an infant or to expose it to cold and starvation and the dogs; even an adult would prefer to die by the sword. But for us, to whom homicide has been once for all forbidden, it is not permitted to break up even what has been conceived in the womb . . . Prevention of birth is premature murder . . . When you are putting Christians to the test you offer them sausages filled with blood, being of course, quite sure that the means by which you would have them deviate from their faith is to them a thing impermissible. How absurd it is for you to believe that they are panting for the blood of man, when to your own knowledge they abhor the blood of beasts. (*Translation by F. A. Wright,* Fathers of the Church, London: Routledge & Kegan Paul Ltd.)

ATHEISM: *Justin in his* First Apology *pointed to the "atheism" of Socrates, partly as a tactical device, but also because he believed Socrates and others among the Greeks to have been inspired by the logos which became later incarnate in Christ:*

When Socrates endeavored by true reason and examination . . . to deliver men from demons, then the demons themselves, by means of men who rejoiced in iniquity, compassed his death, as an atheist and a profane person, on the charge that 'he was introducing new divini-

ties,' and in our case they display a similar activity. . . .
We confess that we are atheists, so far as gods of this
sort are concerned, but not with respect to the most true
God, the Father of righteousness and temperance and the
other virtues, who is free from all impurity. (*Chapters
V-VI, ANF 1, p. 164.*)

Tatian in his Address to the Greeks *brought the coun-
tercharge of the immoralities of the pagan gods:*

There are legends of the metamorphosis of men: with
you the gods also are metamorphosed. Rhea becomes a
tree: Zeus a dragon. . . . A god becomes a swan, or
takes the form of an eagle, and, making Ganymede his
cupbearer, glories in a vile affection. How can I reverence
gods who are eager for presents and angry if they do not
receive them, . . . How was the dead Antinoüs fixed
as a beautiful youth in the moon? Who carried him
thither? . . . Why have you robbed God? Why do you
dishonor His workmanship? You sacrifice a sheep, and
you adore the same animal. The Bull is in the heavens
and you slaughter its image. . . . The eagle that devours
the man-maker Prometheus is honored, forsooth because
it was an adulterer. (*Chapter X, ANF II, 69.*)

Arnobius in his Against the Heathen *ridiculed the in-
anities and inconsistencies of the gods:*

Pellonia is a goddess strong and mighty to expel enemies. If you do not mind, tell us whose enemies. Two
sides meet. . . . Whom then will Polonia expel, since
both will be fighting? . . . Lateranus, the Brick God, is,
as you say, the divinity of hearths and their guardian
spirit; and he got his name from the fact that men build
fireplaces of this kind with unbaked bricks. Well, suppose a hearth is made of tiles or any other material, will
it not have a guardian spirit? . . . You have a military
Venus—have you not?—who presides over the debauch-
ery of youths and the vices rife in a soldiers' camp. . . .
Ossipago, the Bonefixer, as you call her, gives firmness
and solidity to the bones of young children; Mellonia is
the strong divinity who holds sway over bees, carefully
guarding the sweetness of their honey. Tell me, please,
if there were no bees at all on earth, would there be no
goddess Mellonia? . . . Why should there be a god in

charge of honey only? Why should there not be one also for marrows, marjoram, cress, figs, beets and cabbages? (*Chapter IV, 1-10, translation F. A. Wright, op. cit.*)

ALOOFNESS: *Tertullian in his* Apology *specifies what Christians will and will not do in company with their pagan neighbors:*

If we are bidden to love our enemies, whom have we to hate? Again, if when we are injured we are forbidden to retaliate lest by such action we should fall to our enemy's level, whom can we injure? Look at the facts yourselves. . . . How often does the hostile rabble take the law into its own hands and attack us with stones and fires? . . . Yet what instance did you ever note of our retaliation upon you for the injuries inflicted upon us? . . . We are but of yesterday, and yet we have filled all that is yours, cities, islands, forts, country towns, assemblies, camps even, tribes, councils, the palace, the senate, the forum; we have left you only the temples. . . . If such a mass of men as we had broken off from you and removed ourselves to some distant corner of the world, the loss of so many citizens would assuredly have abashed your rule, nay, rather would have punished it by the mere fact of abandonment. Without doubt you would have quaked at your loneliness, at the silence of your business, and the death-like stupefaction of the world. You would have had to look for subjects to rule. . . . You have preferred to call [*the Christians*] enemies of the human race rather than enemies of human error. And yet who but we could have rescued you from those secret enemies that everywhere play havoc with your minds and health, I mean the attack of evil spirits?

Moreover, ought you not to have shown some leniency and enrolled our sect among those associations that the law allows, seeing that it commits none of the offences that are usually to be feared from illegal clubs? . . . Nothing is more foreign to us than politics. We recognize but one state, the world, and that is common to us all.

As for your public shows, we renounce them as completely as we renounce their origin. . . . We have nothing to say or see or hear in connection with the frenzy of the circus, the shamelessness of the theatre, the cruelty of the arena, and the folly of the gymnasium. In what do we offend you, if we prefer different pleasures? . . .

I will now at once proceed to explain the actual occupations of the Christian association, and having refuted the idea that they are evil will show that they are good. We are a corporation based on consciousness of religion, unity of discipline, and partnership in hope. We come together in congregation for meeting, so that forming in a band, as it were, we may draw near to God and surround him with prayers and supplications. This violence is pleasing to God. We pray, too, for emperors, for their ministers and those in authority, for the state of the world, for the peace of the empire, and for the postponement of the end. We come together for the recital of Scripture. . . . Our assembly also is the place of exhortation, correction, and godly criticism.

Even if we have a kind of treasury, this is not filled up by fees paid as the purchase money of religion. Each of us contributes a small sum once a month or when he pleases, and only if he is both willing and able. No one is forced; contributions are voluntary and are regarded as pious investments. The money is not disbursed uselessly on banquets or drinking bouts, but on the feeding and burying of the poor, on boys and girls without means or parents, on old servants and shipwrecked persons, and on any who are in the mines and prisons, they thus becoming pensioners of their own confession of faith.

It is the working of this kind of love that brands us most deeply in some people's eyes. 'See,' they say, 'how they love one another!' (*Chapters XXXVII-XXXIX, translation by F. A. Wright, op. cit.*)

The Quality of Christian Living *is a frequent theme in the Apologists. The following excerpts are from Origen* Against Celsus:

We affirm that the whole human world has evidence of the work of Jesus since in it dwell the churches of God which consist of people converted through Jesus from countless evils. Moreover, the name of Jesus still takes away mental distractions from men, and demons and diseases as well, and implants a wonderful meekness and tranquility of character, and a love to mankind and a kindness and gentleness, in those who have not feigned to be Christians on account of their need of the necessities of life or some other want, but have genuinely accepted the gospel about God and Christ and the judgment to come. (I:67.)

But God, who sent Jesus, destroyed the whole conspiracy of demons, and everywhere in the world in order that men might be converted and reformed He made the gospel of Jesus to be successful, and caused churches to exist in opposition to the assemblies of superstitious, licentious, and unrighteous men. For such is the character of the crowds who everywhere constitute the assemblies of the cities. And the Churches of God which have been taught by Christ, when compared with the assemblies of the people where they live, are 'as lights in the world.' Who would not admit that even the less satisfactory members of the Church and those who are far inferior when compared with the better members are far superior to the assemblies of the people? (III:29.)

The Historical Influence of Jesus *was cited by Origen in the* Against Celsus *as evidence of his divine power:*

If one were also to inquire further into the circumstances of such a man, how could one help trying to find out how a man, brought up in meanness and poverty, who had no general education and had learnt no arguments and doctrines by which he could have become a persuasive speaker to crowds and a popular leader and have won over many hearers, could devote himself to teaching new doctrines and introduce to mankind a doctrine which did away with the customs of the Jews while reverencing their prophets, and which abolished the laws of the Greeks particularly in respect of the worship of God? How could such a man, brought up in this way, who had received no serious instruction from men (as even those who speak evil of him admit), say such noble utterances about the judgment of God, about the punishments for wickedness, and rewards for goodness, that not only rustic and illiterate people were converted by his words, but also a considerable number of the more intelligent, whose vision could penetrate the veil of apparently quite simple expressions, which conceals within itself, as one might say, a more mysterious interpretation?

The Seriphian in Plato reproached Themistocles after he had become famous for his generalship, saying that he had not won his fame by his own character, but from the good luck to have had the most famous city in all Greece as his home. From Themistocles, who was open-minded and saw that his home had also contributed to his fame, he received the answer: 'I would never have been so famous if I had been a Seriphian, nor would you have been a Themistocles if you had had the good luck to be an Athenian.' But our Jesus, who is reproached for having come from a village, and that not a Greek one, who did not belong to any nation prominent in public opinion, and who is maligned as the son of a poor woman who earned her living by spinning and as having left his home country on account of poverty and hired himself out as a workman in Egypt, was not just a Seriphian, to take the illustration I have quoted, but was a Seriphian of the very lowest class, if I may say so. Yet he has been able to shake the whole human world, not only more than Themistocles the Athenian, but even more than Pythagoras and Plato and any other wise men or emperors or generals in any part of the world. (*1:29 translations by Chadwick.*)

— Reading No. 4 —

RIVAL RELIGIONS

I. The Mysteries

The initiation of Lucius in the cult of Isis from The Metamorphoses, *formerly called* The Golden Ass *of Apuleius from the translation of William Adlington done in 1566 and reprinted at London in 1904 at the Chiswick Press for George Bell and Sons. The excerpts are from the eleventh book.*

Lucius by dabbling in magic was accidentally turned into an ass. Sleeping on the warm sand by the seashore about the first watch of the night he awoke in sudden terror as he saw the full moon with unusual splendor emerging from the waves. This was the hour, he knew, when the goddess Isis exercised her greatest power.

The Supplication to Isis: *To her he addressed a prayer that he be restored to his pristine shape.*

❧   ❧   ❧

When I had ended this orayson, and discovered my plaintes to the Goddesse, I fortuned to fall a sleepe, and by and by appeared to me a divine and venerable face, woorshipped even of the Goddes them selves: Then by litle and litle I seemed to see the whole figure of her bodie, mountinge out of the sea and standinge before me: wherefore I purpose to describe her divine semblaunce, if the povertie of my humaine speach will suffer me, or her divine power give me eloquence thereto. First she had a great abondance of heare, disparsed and scattered about her necke, on the crowne of her head she bare many garlandes enterlaced with flowres, in the middle of her forehead, was a compasse

124

in fashion of a glasse, or resembling the light of the
moone, in one of her hands she bare serpentes, in the
other blades of corne, her vestment was of fine silke
yelding divers colours, sometime white, sometime yel-
low, sometime rosie, sometime flamy, and sometime
(which troubled my spirit sore) darke and obscure
covered with a blacke robe in manner of a shield, and
pleatted in most subtill fashion, at the skirties of her
garment, the weltes appeared comely, where as here
and there the starres glimpsed, and in the middle of
them was placed the Moone, which shone like a flame
of fire, round about the robe was a coron or garlande
made with flowers and fruictes: In her right hande
she had a timbrel of brasse which gave a pleasaunt
sounde, in her left hande she bare a cuppe of golde,
out of the mouth whereof the serpent Aspis lifted up
his head, with a swellinge throate, her odoriferous feete
were covered with shoes enterlaced and wrought with
victorious palme. Thus the divine shape breathing out
the pleasant spice of fertil Arabia, dayned not with her
divine voice to utter these woordes unto me: Beholde
Lucius I am come, thy weeping and prayers hath
moved me to succour thee.

*Isis instructed Lucius during her rites to eat a garland of
roses carried by her priest. This he did and was restored
to human form. In gratitude he became an initiate of her
cult and describes below as much as he was permitted to
disclose of his induction.*

. . . thou shalt understande that I approched nere unto
Hell, even to the gates of Proserpina, and after that I
was ravished throughout all the Elementes, I returned
to my proper place: About midnight I sawe the sonne
shine, I saw likewise the Goddes celestiall, and Goddes
infernall, before whome I presented my selfe and woorshipped them: beholde now have I tolde thee, which
although thou hast harde, yet it is necessary that you
conceale it, for this have I declared without offence, for
the understanding of the prophane. When morninge
came and that the solempnities were finished, I came
foorth sanctified with twelve Stoles and in a religious

habite, wherof I am not forbidden to speake, consideringe that many persons sawe me at that time: there I was commaunded to stande uppon a seate of woodde which stoode in the middle of the temple, before the figure and remembraunce of the Goddesse, my vestment was of fine linnen, covered and embrodered with flowres, I had a pretious cope upon my shoulders hanginge downe to the grounde, whereon were beastes wrought of divers colours, as Indian Dragons, and Hyperborian Gryphones, whome in forme of birdes the other world doth engender, the Priestes commonly call such a habit, a celestiall Stole: in my right hande I carried a light torche, and a garland of flowres upon my head, with Palme leaves stroutinge out on every side: I was adorned like unto the Sunne, and made in fashion of an Image, in such sorte that all the people compassed about to beholde me: Then they beganne to solemnise the feast of my nativitie, and the newe procession with sumptuous bankets and delicate meates: the thirde day was likewise celebrate with like ceremonies, with a religious dinner, and with all the consummation of the order, when I had continued there a good space I conceaved a mervelous pleasure and consolation in beholding ordinarily the Image of the goddesse, who at length admonished me to departe homewarde, not without rendringe of thankes, whiche although were not sufficient, yet they were according to my power: How be it I could unneth [scarcely] be perswaded to depart, before I had fallen prostrate before the face of the Goddesse, and wiped her steppes [feet] with my face, whereby I beganne so greatly to weepe and sighe, that my woordes were interrupted, and as devouring my prayer I began to say in this sorte: O holy and blessed Dame, the perpetuall comfort of humaine kinde, who by thy bountie and grace nourishest all the world, and bearest a great affection to the adversities of the miserable as a loving mother, thou takest no rest, neyther arte thou idle at any time in givinge thy benefites, and succoringe all men aswell on lande as sea, thou arte she that puttest away all stormes and daungers from mans life by thy right hande, whereby likewise thou restraynest the fatall dispositions, appeasest the great tempestes of fortunes, and keepest backe the course of the starres, the Gods supernall doth honour thee, the Gods infernall hath thee in reverence, thou environest al the worlde, thou givest light to the Sunne, thou governest the world, thou treadest downe the power of Hell: By thy meane the times returne, the Planets rejoyse, the Elementes serve: at thy commaundement the windes doo blowe, the cloudes encrease, the seedes prosper, and the fruictes prevayle, the birdes of the ayre, the beastes of the hill, the Serpentes of the denne, and the fishes of the sea, doo tremble at thy majestie, but my spirite is not able to give thee sufficient prayse, my patrimonie is unable to satisfie thy sacrifice, my voyce hath no power to utter that which I thinke, no if I had a thousande mouthes and so many tongues: How be it as a good religious personne, and according to my estate, I wil alwaies keepe thee in remembraunce, and close thee within my brest. When I had ended mine orayson, I wente to embrase the great Prieste Mithra my spirituall Father and to demaunde his pardon, considering I was unable to recompence the good whiche he had done me: After great greetinges and thankes I departed from him to visitte my parents and freendes. And within a while after by the exhortation of the Goddesse, I made up my packquette and toke shippyng towardes the Citie of Rome, where, with a prosperous winde I arrived about the twelfe day of December.

II. Gnosticism

A. Valentinus

In 1946 a jar of Gnostic papyri was discovered in upper Egypt. The material dates from about the middle of the fourth century. The language is Coptic but the original was manifestly Greek. One tract bears the title The Gospel of Truth. *This is the title of a lost work known to have been written by the Gnostic Valentinus, but the treatise does not contain the doctrine ascribed to him by the Church Fathers of a system of aeons emanating from the abyss. Perhaps they were describing another phase of his thought or perhaps the system of his follow-*

ers. The translation is from Evangelium Veritatis *(Codex Jung), ed. Michel Malinine, Henri-Charles Puech, and Gilles Quispel (Zürich: Rascher Verlag, 1956). Excerpts follow:*

✓   ✓   ✓

The Gospel of Truth is joy for those who have received the grace of knowing from the Father of Truth Him through the power of the Verb, come forth from the Pleroma, who is immanent in the Thought and in the Mind of the Father and who is He whom they call "The Saviour," for that is the name of the work which He is to accomplish for the Salvation of those who were ignorant of the Father. . . . The Gospel is a revelation of Hope, since it is a discovery for those who seek Him. Indeed the All was searching for Him from whom it came forth. But the All was inside of Him that Incomprehensible, Inconceivable (One), who is superior to all thought. It was this ignorance concerning the Father which produced Anguish and Terror. And Anguish became dense like a mist, so that no one could see. For this reason error was strengthened. It elaborated its own matter in emptiness, without knowing Truth. It applied itself to the modeling of a creature trying to provide in beauty the equivalent of Truth. This, then, was not a humiliation for Him, that Incomprehensible, Inconceivable (One). . . . For they were as nothing, (namely) that Anguish and Oblivion and that creature of Falsehood, whereas this established Truth is inalterable, unshakable and of a perfect beauty. For this reason despise error. . . . Oblivion did not exist close to the Father although It came into existence because of Him. On the contrary, that which comes into existence because in Him is Knowledge (the Gnose), which appeared in order that Oblivion should be abolished and in order that they might know the Father. Since Oblivion came into existence because they did not know the Father, therefore if they attain to a knowledge of the Father, Oblivion becomes, at that very instant, non-existent. That, then, is the Gospel of Him whom they seek and which He revealed to the Perfect, thanks to the clemency of the Father, as a hidden mystery, He, Jesus, the Christ. . . . He came in a similitude of Flesh, although nothing could obstruct Its course, because It was incorruptible and uncoercable. Moreover, pronouncing new things, saying that which is in the heart of the Father, He proclaimed the Word which is without flaw. Light spoke through His mouth, and His voice engendered Life. . . . He became a Way for those who erred, and a Gnose for those who were ignorant; a Discovery for those who sought and a Confirmation for those who vacillated; an immaculate Innocence for those who were defiled. He is a Shepherd who abandoned the ninety-nine lambs who had not strayed. He went in search of the one which was lost. . . . All the beings which have emanated from the Father are Pleromas. . . . Neither have they been deprived of the Glory of the Father. . . . This is the manner of existence of those who have something from on high, near that immeasurable Grandeur, while they strain towards that unique One who is perfect and who is there for their sakes. And they do not descend into Hades. They experience neither desire nor lamentation; no more is there Death in them. But it is in Him who is in repose that they repose, without striving nor becoming entangled in the search for Truth. But they are themselves Truth; and the Father is in them, and they are in the Father.

B. Marcion

Marcion broke with the Roman church in A.D. *144. The following excerpts are from Tertullian,* Against Marcion *Book V, 5; Book 1, 24; Book III, 8; and Book 1, 29. They are translated in ANF III, pp. 440, 290, 327 and 294. According to Tertullian, Marcion identified the God of the Old Testament with the Demiurge, the creator of this evil world.*

✦   ✦   ✦

Rejection of the Old Testament. The very Old Testament of the Creator itself, it is possible, no doubt to charge with foolishness, and weakness, and dishonor, and meanness and contempt. What is more foolish and more weak than God's requirement of bloody sacrifices and of savory holocausts? What is weaker than the cleansing of vessels and of beds? What more dishonourable than the discoloration of the reddening skin? What so mean as the statute of retaliation? What so contemptible as the exception in meats and drinks? The whole of the Old Testament, the heretic, to the best of my belief, holds in derision.

Marcion held that the God and Father of Jesus Christ delivered mankind from the sway of the Creator. Tertullian pointed out that the deliverance was very imperfect.

Poor dupe of Marcion, fever is hard upon you; and your painful flesh produces a crop of all sorts of briars and thorns. Nor is it only to the Creator's thunderbolts that you lie exposed, or to wars, and pestilences, and His other heavier strokes, but even to His creeping insects. In what respect do you suppose yourself liberated from His kingdom when His flies are still creeping upon your face? If your deliverance lies in the future, why not also in the present, that it may be perfectly wrought? Far different is our condition in the sight of Him who is the Author, the Judge, the injured Head of our race! You display Him as a merely good God; but you are unable to prove that He is perfectly good, because you are not by Him perfectly delivered.

Marcion took a docetic view of Christ denying the reality of his earthly body. Tertullian answered:

Docetism. He alleges Christ to be a phantom. . . . His Christ in order to avoid the imputation, if possible, of belonging to the Creator, was not what he appeared to be, and feigned himself to be what he was not—incarnate without being flesh, human without being man, and likewise a divine Christ without being God. . . . Since, however, Christ's being flesh is now discovered to be a lie, it follows that all things which were done by the flesh of Christ were done untruly. . . . On this principle the sufferings of Christ will be found not to warrant faith in him. For he suffered nothing who did not truly suffer; and a phantom could not really suffer. God's entire work, therefore, is subverted. Christ's death, wherein lies the whole weight and fruit of the Christian name, is denied.

Marcion condemned marriage and would baptize only those who were at the time unmarried. Tertullian replied:

Marriage: [*God*] bestowed His blessing on matrimony also, as on an honourable estate, for the increase of the human race; . . . To put a complete stop, however, to the sowing of the human race, may, for aught I know, be quite consistent for Marcion's most good and excellent god. For how could he desire the salvation of man, whom he forbids to be born, when he takes away that institution from which his birth arises?

How will he find any one on whom to set the mark of his goodness, when he suffers him not to come into existence? How is it possible to love him whose origin he hates? Perhaps he is afraid of a redundant population, lest he should be weary in liberating so many;

The cruelty of Pharaoh, which slew its victims at their birth, will not prove to be more inhuman in comparison. For while he destroyed lives, our heretic's god refuses to give them.

THE CONSOLIDATION OF THE CHURCH

I. The Canon of Scripture

The Muratorian fragment, named for its discoverer Muratori, describes the books acknowledged by the Roman Church about A.D. *170. The* Wisdom of Solomon *belongs to the Old Testament* Apocrypha *consisting of the books in Greek and not in Hebrew. The* Apocalypse of John (*our Revelation*) *was subsequently received but the* Apocalypse of Peter *was rejected. The translation is from J. Stevenson,* A New Eusebius (*Loeb Library, 1957*), *No. 124.*

✓   ✓   ✓

. . . but at some he was present, and so he set them down [*referring to Mark*].

The third book of the Gospel, that according to Luke, was compiled in his own name on Paul's authority by Luke the physician, when after Christ's ascension Paul had taken him to be with him like a legal expert. Yet neither did he see the Lord in the flesh; and he too, as he was able to ascertain events, begins his story from the birth of John.

The fourth of the Gospels was written by John, one of the disciples. When exhorted by his fellow-disciples and bishops, he said, 'Fast with me this day for three days; and what may be revealed to any of us, let us relate it to one another.' The same night it was revealed to Andrew, one of the apostles, that John was to write all things in his own name, and they were all to certify.

And therefore, though various ideas are taught in the several books of the Gospels, yet it makes no difference to the faith of believers, since by one sovereign Spirit all things are declared in all of them concerning the Nativity, the Passion, the Resurrection, the conversation with his disciples and his two comings, the first in lowliness and contempt, which has come to pass, the second glorious with royal power, which is to come.

What marvel therefore if John so firmly sets forth each statement in his Epistles too, saying of himself, "What we have seen with our eyes and heard with our ears and our hands have handled, these things we have written to you"? For so he declares himself not an eyewitness and a hearer only, but a writer of all the marvels of the Lord in order.

The Acts, however, of all the Apostles are written in one book. Luke, to the most excellent Theophilus, includes events because they were done in his own presence, as he also plainly shows by leaving out the passion of Peter, and also the departure of Paul from the City on his journey to Spain.

The Epistles, however, of Paul themselves make plain to those who wish to understand it, what epistles were sent by him, and from what place or for what cause. He wrote at some length first of all to the Corinthians, forbidding the schisms of heresy; next to the Galatians, forbidding circumcision; then he wrote to the Romans at greater length, impressing on them the rule of the Scriptures, and also that Christ is the first principle of them, concerning which severally it is not necessary for us to discuss. For the blessed Apostle Paul himself, following the rule of his predecessor John, writes only by name to seven churches in the following order—to the Corinthians a first, to the Ephesians a second, to the Philippians a third, to the Colossians a fourth, to the Galatians a fifth, to the Thessalonians a sixth, to the Romans a seventh; although for the sake of admonition there is a second to the Corinthians and to the Thessalonians, yet one Church is recognized as being spread over the entire world. For John too in the Apocalypse, though he writes to seven churches, yet speaks to all. Howbeit to Philemon one, to Titus one, and to Timothy two were put in writing from personal inclination and attachment, to be in honour however with the Catholic Church for the ordering of ecclesiastical discipline. There is in circulation also one to the

Laodicenes, another to the Alexandrians, both forged in
Paul's name to suit the heresy of Marcion, and several
others, which cannot be received into the Catholic Church;
for it is not fitting that gall be mixed with honey.

The Epistle of Jude no doubt, and the couple bearing
the name of John, are accepted in the Catholic Church;
and the Wisdom written by the friends of Solomon in his
honour. The Apocalypse also of John, and of Peter only
we receive, which some of our friends will not have read
in the Church. But the Shepherd was written quite lately
in our times in the city of Rome by Hermas, while his
brother Pius, the bishop, was sitting in the chair of the
church of the city of Rome; and therefore it ought indeed
to be read, but it cannot to the end of time be publicly
read in the Church to the people, either among the
prophets, who are complete in number, or among the
Apostles.

But of Arsinous, called also Valentinus, or of Miltiades
we receive nothing at all; those who have also composed
a new book of Psalms for Marcion, together with Basil-
eides and the Asian founder of the Cataphrygians are
rejected.

II. Tradition Localized in the Episcopacy through
Apostolic Succession

A. Apostolic Succession. *From Clement of Rome writing
to the church at Corinth about* A.D. *95, Sections 42 and
44, translated by Kirsopp Lake in* The Apostolic Fathers,
Loeb Library.

✓   ✓   ✓

The Apostles received the Gospel for us from the Lord
Jesus Christ, Jesus the Christ was sent from God. The
Christ therefore is from God and the Apostles from the
Christ. In both ways, then, they were in accordance with
the appointed order of God's will. Having therefore received their commands, and being fully assured by the
resurrection of our Lord Jesus Christ, and with faith confirmed by the word of God, they sent forth in the assurance of the Holy Spirit preaching the good news that the
Kingdom of God is coming. They preached from district

to district, and from city to city, and they appointed their first converts, testing them by the Spirit, to be bishops and deacons of the future believers. And this was no new method, for many years before had bishops and deacons been written of; for the scripture says thus in one place 'I will establish their bishops in righteousness, and their deacons in faith.' . . .

Our Apostles also knew through our Lord Jesus Christ that there would be strife for the title of bishop. For this cause, therefore, since they had received perfect foreknowledge, they appointed those who have been already mentioned, and afterwards added the codicil that if they should fall asleep, other approved men should succeed to their ministry. We consider therefore that it is not just to remove from their ministry those who were appointed by them, or later on by other eminent men, with the consent of the whole Church, and have ministered to the flock of Christ without blame, humbly, peaceably, and disinterestedly, and for many years have received a universally favourable testimony. For our sin is not small, if we eject from the episcopate those who have blamelessly and holily offered its sacrifices. Blessed are those Presbyters who finished their course before now, and have obtained a fruitful and perfect release in the ripeness of completed work, for they have now no fear that any shall move them from the place appointed to them. For we see that in spite of their good service you have removed some from the ministry which they fulfilled blamelessly.

B. The Pre-eminence of the Bishop. *Ignatius of Antioch earlier than* A.D. *117, in his letter* To The Smyrneans, *viii, translated by Kirsopp Lake in the* Apostolic Fathers, *Loeb Library.*

✓   ✓   ✓

See that you all follow the bishop, as Jesus Christ follows the Father, and the presbytery as if it were the Apostles. And reverence the deacons as the command of God. Let no one do any of the things appertaining to the Church without the bishop. Let that be considered a valid Eucharist which is celebrated by the bishop, or by one whom he appoints. Wherever the bishop appears let the congregation be present; just as wherever Jesus Christ is, there is the Catholic Church. It is not lawful either to baptise or to hold an "agapë" without the bishop; but whatever he approve, this is also pleasing to God, that everything which you do may be secure and valid.

C. Tradition and Episcopacy. *Irenaeus* Against Heresies, *iii, 1-4, translated in James Shotwell and Louise Loomis,* The See of Peter (*New York; Columbia University Press, 1927), pp. 265-71.*

✓   ✓   ✓

Now we have learned the plan of our salvation entirely from the men through whom the gospel came to us. For at first they proclaimed it abroad and afterwards, by the will of God, they set it down for us in the Scriptures to be the foundation and pillar of our faith. It is wicked to say, as some venture to do who boast that they improve upon the apostles, that the latter preached before they had attained to "perfect knowledge." For after our Lord arose from the dead and they were filled with the power of the Holy Ghost descending from on high, they were complete every whit and had perfect knowledge; . . . [*They wrote the gospels: Matthew, Mark, Luke and John.*]

But when these people [*the Gnostics*] are refuted out of the Scriptures, they turn and accuse the Scriptures themselves, on the ground that they are mistaken or not authoritative or not consistent in their wording, and they say that the truth cannot be learned from them by persons who do not know the tradition, for that was not transmitted in writing but by word of mouth. . . .

Then when we challenge them again with the tradition which comes from the apostles and is preserved in the churches by the presbyters in their successions, they attack the tradition and insist that they are wiser not only than the presbyters but even than the apostles and that they have discovered the unalloyed truth. . . .

Now it is within the power of anyone, who cares, to find out the truth and to know the tradition of the apostles, professed throughout the world in every church. We are also able to name those who were appointed bishops by the apostles in the churches and their successors down to our own times. They neither taught nor knew of any such thing as these hallucinations. Yet, if the apostles had been aware of any hidden mysteries, which were disclosed to "the prefect" apart and secretly from the rest, they would have delivered them first of all to the men to whom they committed the churches. For they desired above all that these men should be perfect and blameless in everything, since they were leaving them behind as their successors and entrusting their own office of government to them, so that if they walked uprightly, it would be of great benefit, and if they fell away, a dire calamity.

But inasmuch as it would be very tedious in a book such as this to rehearse the lines of succession in every church, we will put to confusion all persons who, whether from waywardness or vainglory or blindness or perversity of mind, combine wrongfully together in any way, by pointing to the tradition, derived from the apostles, of that great and illustrious church founded and organized at Rome by the two glorious apostles, Peter and Paul, and to the faith declared to mankind and handed down to our own time through its bishops in their succession. For unto this church, on account of its commanding position, every church, that is to say, the faithful from everywhere, must needs resort and in it the tradition that comes from the apostles has been continuously preserved by those who are from everywhere.

The blessed apostles then founded and reared up this church and afterwards committed unto Linus the office of the episcopate. This same Linus is mentioned by Paul in his epistles to Timothy. His successor was Anacletus, after whom in the third place from the apostles, Clement was elected to the bishopric.

To this Clement succeeded Evaristus and Evaristus was followed by Alexander. Then, sixth after the apostles, Sixtus held office; after him Telesphorus, who was a glorious martyr; next Hyginus, then Pius, and after Pius, Anicetus. Soter succeeded Anicetus and now, in the twelfth place from the apostles, Eleutherus has the office of the episcopate. In this order and by this succession the tradition of the apostles in the Church and the preaching of the truth have passed down to us. And herein is abundant proof that the lifegiving faith is one and the same which has been preserved in the Church from the apostles until now and handed on in truth.

Seeing, therefore, that we have such testimony, we do not need to seek elsewhere the truth which it is easy to find in the Church. For the apostles, like a rich man at a bank, deposited lavishly with her all aspects of the truth, so that everyone, whoever will, may draw from her the water of life. For she is the door to life and all others are thieves and robbers. For this reason we ought to shun them and love the things of the Church with utmost diligence and lay hold of the tradition of the truth. What more? Suppose that a disagreement on some important question arises among us, must we not then have recourse to the most ancient churches, with whom the apostles lived, and ascertain from them what is positive and clear in regard to the question in dispute? What if the apostles had left us no Scriptures, would it not then be required of us to follow the course of the tradition which they bequeathed to the men to whom they committed the churches?

III. The Formulation of Dogma

A. The Statement at Baptism. *from* The Apostolic Tradition of Hippolytus, *translated by Burton S. Easton* (*New York: Cambridge University Press, 1934*) *pp. 46-47.*

✓   ✓   ✓

At cockcrow prayer shall be made over the water. The stream shall flow through the baptismal tank or pour into it from above when there is no scarcity of water; but if there is a scarcity, whether constant or sudden, then use whatever water you can find.

They shall remove their clothing. And first baptize the little ones; if they can speak for themselves, they shall do so; if not, their parents or other relatives shall speak for them. Then baptize the men, and last of all the women; they must first loosen their hair and put aside any gold or silver ornaments that they were wearing: let no one take any alien thing down to the water with them.

At the hour set for the baptism the bishop shall give

thanks over oil and put it into a vessel: this is called the "oil of thanksgiving." And he shall take other oil and exorcise it: this is called "the oil of exorcism." [*The anointing is performed by a presbyter.*] A deacon shall bring the oil of exorcism, and shall stand at the presbyter's left hand; and another deacon shall take the oil of thanksgiving, and shall stand at the presbyter's right hand. Then the presbyter, taking hold of each of those about to be baptized, shall command him to renounce, saying:

I renounce thee, Satan, and all thy servants and all thy works.

And when he has renounced all these, the presbyter shall anoint him with the oil of exorcism, saying:

Let all spirits depart far from thee.

Then, after these things, let him give him over to the presbyter who baptizes, and let the candidates stand in the water, naked, a deacon going with them likewise. And when he who is being baptized goes down into the water, he who baptizes him, putting his hand on him, shall say thus:

Dost thou believe in God, the Father Almighty?

And he who is being baptized shall say:

I believe.

Then holding his hand placed on his head, he shall baptize him once. And then he shall say:

Dost thou believe in Christ Jesus, the Son of God, who was born of the Holy Ghost of the Virgin Mary, and was crucified under Pontius Pilate, and was dead and buried, and rose again the third day, alive from the dead, and ascended into heaven, and sat at the right hand of the Father, and will come to judge the quick and the dead?

And when he says:

I believe,

he is baptized again. And again he shall say:

Dost thou believe in [*the*] Holy Ghost, and the holy church, and the resurrection of the flesh?

He who is being baptized shall say accordingly:

I believe,

and so he is baptized a third time.

And afterward, when he has come up [*out of the water*], he is anointed by the presbyter with the oil of thanksgiving, the presbyter saying:

I anoint thee with holy oil in the name of Jesus Christ. And so each one, after drying himself, is immediately clothed, and then is brought into the church.

B. The Old Roman Symbol, *in Philip Schaff* The Creeds of Christendom, *4th ed.* (*3 vols.*) *New York: Harpers, 1890.* (*II, pp. 47-48.*)

I believe in God the Father almighty;
And in Jesus Christ His only Son, our Lord;
Who was born of the Holy Ghost and the Virgin Mary;
Crucified under Pontius Pilate and buried;
The third day rose again from the dead;
He ascended into heaven,
And sitteth at the right hand of the Father;
From thence he shall come to judge the quick and the dead.
In the Holy Ghost;
The holy Church;
The forgiveness of sins;
The resurrection of the body;
(The life everlasting) [*in the Greek*].

C. The Apostles' Creed. *The Received Form. Translated in Schaff, op. cit., p. 46.*

The descent into hell has reference to the deliverance of the spirits there imprisoned before the coming of Christ. The term Catholic as applied to the Church meant originally universal, but was coming to mean orthodox. The communion of saints refers presumably to communion with the departed. The forgiveness of sins asserts the right of the Church to forgive sins. The resurrection of the body was directed against Gnostic tendencies but did not mean that every bone would rise again. The Apostle Paul said that the resurrection body is a spiritual body.

I believe in God the Father Almighty; Maker of heaven and earth. And in Jesus Christ his only Son our Lord; who was conceived by the Holy Ghost, born of the Virgin Mary; suffered under Pontius Pilate, was crucified, dead, and buried; he descended into hell; the third day he rose from the dead; he ascended into heaven; and sitteth at the right hand of God the Father Almighty; from thence he shall come to judge the quick and the dead. I believe in the Holy Ghost; the holy Catholic Church; the communion of saints; the forgiveness of sins; the resurrection of the body, and the life everlasting. Amen.

— Reading No. 6 —

THE ESTABLISHMENT OF DISCIPLINE

I. Forgiveness of Sins after Baptism

From Hermas, The Shepherd, *vis. 11, ii, 4-8, translated by Kirsopp Lake in* The Apostolic Fathers, *Loeb Library.*

✶   ✶   ✶

The Master commanded me to reveal to you, all the sins which they have formerly committed shall be forgiven them, and they shall be forgiven to all the saints who have sinned up to this day, if they repent with their whole heart, and put aside double-mindedness from their heart. For the Master has sworn to his elect by his glory that if there be still sin after this day has been fixed, they shall find no salvation; for repentance for the just has an end; the days of repentance have been fulfilled for all the saints, but for the heathen repentance is open until the last day. You shall say, then, to the leaders of the Church, that they reform their ways in righteousness, to receive in full the promises with great glory. You, therefore, 'who work righteousness,' must remain steadfast and be not double-minded, that your passing may be with the holy angels. Blessed are you, as many as endure the great persecution which is coming, and as many as shall not deny their life. For the Lord has sworn by his Son that those who have denied their Christ have been rejected from their life, that is, those who shall now deny him in the days to come. But those who denied him formerly have obtained forgiveness through his great mercy.

142

II. Forgiveness of Sexual Offenses

A. The Ruling of Callistus, *from Tertullian* On Modesty, *translated in Shotwell and Loomis,* op. cit., p. 301.

✝ ✝ ✝

. . . I hear also that there has been published an edict and a peremptory one too. The Pontifex Maximus, that is, the bishop of the bishops, has issued a decree. "I remit to such as have done penance the sins of adultery and fornication." O edict that cannot be called "approved"! Where shall this liberality be posted up? On the spot, I should suppose; directly on the gates of lust, beneath the roofs dedicated to it! That is the place for publishing such a penance, where the sin itself makes its home. That is the place for reading the pardon, where men enter confidently expecting it. But this edict is read in church and proclaimed aloud in church, although the Church is virgin. Away, away, with such displays from the bride of Christ.

So produce anew for me, O successor of the apostles, your examples from the prophets and I will admit the right divine. But you arrogate to yourself the vast power of forgiveness of sins, although what you have is only the duty of maintaining discipline, not the headship of an empire but of a ministry. Who and what are you to show mercy, who conduct yourself neither as prophet nor as apostle and are destitute of the virtue that is necessary for one who is merciful? "But," you say, "the Church has the power of forgiving sins." If, because the Lord said to Peter: "Upon this rock I will build my Church . . . to thee have I given the keys of the kingdom of heaven," or: "Whatsoever thou shalt bind or loose on earth shall be bound or loosed in heaven," you therefore assume that the power of binding and loosing has descended to you or to any church related to Peter, what sort of man are you, overthrowing and transforming the manifest intention of the Lord, who conferred the gift personally upon Peter? "On thee," he says, "will I build my Church," and "I will give unto thee the keys," not "unto the Church"; and "whatsoever thou shalt loose or bind," not "whatsoever they shall loose or bind."

What now has this to do with the Church and in particular your church, O follower of the Spirit? As this power was conferred upon Peter personally, so it belongs to spiritual men, whether apostle or prophet. For the true Church is by nature and origin the Spirit himself, in whom is the Trinity of the one Godhead, Father, Son and Holy Spirit. He unites together that Church which the Lord made to consist of three. So ever since then, any number of persons who join together in faith is accounted a church by its Author and Consecrator. The Church, indeed, will forgive sins but only the Church of the Spirit, through the voice of a spiritual man, not the Church which is merely a collection of bishops.

B. The Account of Hippolytus. Refutation of All Heresies *IX, 2, 5-7, translated in Shotwell and Loomis, op. cit., pp. 310-11.*

✓   ✓   ✓

[*Callistus*] was the first to devise the idea of indulging men in their pleasures by declaring that he would forgive everyone's sins. So if a man who attends some other congregation and is considered a Christian commits a transgression, his sin, they say, is not reckoned against him, provided he promptly joins the school of Callistus. And numerous persons who had been stricken in conscience and some who had left various heresies and some who had in accordance with our rule, been expelled by us from the church, were relieved at his declaration and united with the rest and crowded his school. He also propounded the view that if a bishop commits sin, even a sin unto death, he need not be deposed. In his time, bishops, priests, and deacons who had been twice or thrice married began to be installed among the clergy and if one of the clergy married, he continued in the clergy as if he had not sinned, for Callistus maintained that with regard to such a man the words of the apostle had been spoken: "Who art thou that judgest another man's servant?" He insisted further that the parable of the tares was intended for such a case. "Let the tares grow together with the wheat!" That is, let the sinners remain in the Church! He likewise said that the ark of Noah was a symbol of the

Church, for in it were dogs, wolves, ravens and everything clean and unclean; and so, he declared, it must also be in the Church. Whatever passages he could collect bearing on this subject he interpreted in this way.

His hearers delight in his teachings and cling to him, deluding themselves, and crowds pour into his school. So they increase in numbers and boast of the multitudes that come in search of pleasures that Christ forbade. In disdain of him they prohibit no sin, proclaiming that Callistus pardons everyone who believes with him. He has even permitted women who were unmarried and were inflamed by passion unfitting to their age or who were unwilling to forfeit their rank by a legal marriage, to have whatever man they chose as concubine, whether he were slave or free, and to regard him as their husband, although they were not legally married to him. . . . [*Further details as to such irregular relations.*] After such brazen conduct these shameless people dare to call themselves a catholic church. And other persons, supposing that they will benefit themselves, join with them. During Callistus' episcopate, they have for the first time presumptuously administered second baptism.

III. Forgiveness of the Lapsed

A. Pardons given by Confessors *from Cyprian,* Epistle *xxvii, 1-2, translated in B. J. Kidd,* Documents Illustrative of the Early Church, *vol. 1 (London: S.P.C.K.),* Doc. *137. The* Request *is from* Epistle *xxiii in Kidd, Doc. 138.*

✦ ✦ ✦

Since my former epistle to you, dearest brethren, in which my conduct was explained, and some slight account given of my discipline and diligence, there hath occurred another matter, of which also you ought not to be uninformed. For our brother Lucianus, himself also one of the Confessors, glowing indeed in faith and strong in courage, but insufficiently grounded in the reading of the word of the Lord, has attempted certain things, making himself for some while past an authority to the ignorant populace, in that letters written in his hand have been given to many persons indiscriminately, in the name of Paulus. Whereas Mappalicus the martyr, being cautious

and modest, regardful of the law and discipline, gave
letters contrary to the Gospel, but, moved by domestic
piety, recommended only that peace should be granted
to his mother [*and sister*] who had lapsed; Saturninus
also, being still in prison, after the torture, issued no
letters of that sort. But Lucianus, not only while Paulus
was still in prison, gave letters in his name indiscriminately written with his own hand; but even after his de-
cease, continued to do the same in his name, saying that
he had been ordered to do so by Paulus; not knowing
that the Lord must rather be obeyed than the fellow-
servant. In the name of Aurelius too, a youth, who has
endured the torture, many letters have been given, written
with the hand of the same Lucianus, because Aurelius
did not know how to write.

To check this practice in some degree, I wrote a letter
which I sent to you under cover of my last Epistle;
wherein I failed not to beg and persuade them, that they
would have regard to the law of the Lord and to the
Gospel. But after I had sent this letter to them, in the
hope that something might be done, as it were more mod-
erately and temperately, the same Lucianus wrote a letter
in the name of all the Confessors, whereby the whole
bond of faith, and the fear of God, and the Commandment of the Lord, and the sanctity and strength of the
Gospel, were well-nigh dissolved. For he wrote in the
name of all, that they had granted peace to all, and that
they wished this sentence to be notified through me to
other Bishops, a copy of which letter I have transmitted
to you.

The Request of the Confessors to Bishop Cyprian

Know that we have granted peace to all of whose behaviour, since the commission of their crime, you are
satisfied; and we desire, through you, to make this known
to other Bishops also. We wish you to maintain peace
with the holy martyrs. Lucianus wrote this; there being
present of the clergy an Exorcist and a Reader.—

B. The Defense of the Libellatici, *that is those who had
accepted certificates of having sacrificed. From Cyprian,*
Epistle *LI, 14,* ANF *V, pp. 330-31.*

✓ ✓ ✓

Since, then, there is much difference between those who have sacrificed, what a want of mercy it is, and how bitter is the hardship, to associate those who have received certificates, with those who have sacrificed, when he by whom the certificate has been received may say, "I had previously read, and had been made aware by the discourse of the bishop, that we must not sacrifice to idols, that the servant of God ought not to worship images; and therefore, in order that I might not do this which was not lawful, when the opportunity of receiving a certificate was offered, which itself also I should not have received, unless the opportunity had been put before me, I either went or charged some other person going to the magistrate, to say that I am a Christian, that I am not allowed to sacrifice, that I cannot come to the devil's altars, and that I pay a price for this purpose, that I may not do what is not lawful for me to do." Now, however, even he who is stained with having received a certificate,—after he has learnt from our admonitions that he ought not even to have done this, and that although his hand is pure, and no contact of deadly food has polluted his lips, yet his conscience is nevertheless polluted, weeps when he hears us, and laments, and is now admonished of the thing wherein he has sinned, and having been deceived, not so much by guilt as by error, bears witness that for another time he is instructed and prepared.

C. The Defence of the Sacrificiati, *who actually had sacrificed, from Cyprian*, On the Lapsed 13, ANF *V, 440.*

✓ ✓ ✓

But (say they) subsequently tortures had come and severe sufferings were threatening those who resisted. He may complain of tortures who has been overcome by tortures; he may offer the excuse of suffering who has been vanquished in suffering. Such a one may ask, and say, "I wished indeed to strive bravely, and, remembering my oath, I took up the arms of devotion and faith; but as I was struggling in the encounter, varied tortures and long-continued sufferings overcame me. My mind stood firm, and my faith was strong, and my soul struggled long, unshaken with the torturing pains; but when, with the renewed barbarity of the most cruel judge, wearied out as I was, the scourges were now tearing me, the clubs bruised me, the rack strained me, the claw dug into me, the fire roasted me; my flesh deserted me in the struggle, the weakness of my bodily frame gave way,—not my mind, but my body, yielded in the suffering." Such a plea may readily avail to forgiveness;

D. The Theory of the Church. *From Cyprian,* On the Unity of the Catholic Church, *translated by F. A. Wright,* op. cit., p. 115.

*   *   *

It is granted that the other apostles were even as Peter was, having an equal share with him of honour and power, but the beginning proceeds from unity. The primacy is given to Peter that it may be shown that the Church is one and the See of Christ is one. All are pastors, but the flock is one, and it is fed by all the pastors in perfect agreement, in order that the unity of Christ's church may be demonstrated. It is this one Church to which the Holy Spirit refers in the Song of Songs, speaking with the voice of the Lord and saying: "My dove, my undefiled, is but one. She is the only one of her mother, elect of her that bore her." He that holds not this unity of the Church, does he think that he holds the true faith? He who resists the Church and contends with it, who abandons the throne of Peter on which the Church is founded, is he confident that he is within the Church? Does not the blessed apostle Paul teach this and prove the doctrine of unity, when he says: "There is one body and one Spirit, one hope of your calling, one Lord, one faith, one baptism, one God."

It is our duty to hold fast this unity and to justify it, especially those of us who are bishops of the Church, that we may show that the episcopate itself also is one and indivisible. Let no man deceive the brethren with false doctrine or destroy faith in the truth by disloyally tampering with it. The episcopate is one, and a part of it is held by each of us, making a complete whole. The Church is one, but with rich exuberance it spreads far and wide among men. Even so there are many rays of the sun, but one sunlight; many branches of a tree, but one trunk firmly grounded in a sound root; and when many streams flow from one spring, although its unity seems to be scattered abroad in the very abundance of the water that flows, yet that unity is preserved in the source. Try to remove one ray of the sun from the whole: the unity of sunlight suffers no division. Break off a branch from a tree: the broken branch will not bud. Cut off a stream from its source: it will dry up. So also the Church of Christ pours forth its light and spreads its rays throughout the whole world; yet it is one light that is everywhere poured forth and the unity of the whole is not destroyed. Or, again, its inexhaustible fertility puts forth branches over the whole world; and like a mighty river it spreads its streams far and wide. But one is the head, one the source, one the mother of abundant and continuous fertility. From her womb we are sprung and reared on her milk, by her breath we are quickened.

The bride of Christ cannot admit of adultery, she is pure and chaste. She knows but one home, and with unbroken chastity she guards one sacred chamber. She it is who preserves us for God, who offers to the Kingdom of God the sons whom she has borne. He that separates himself from the church and makes an adulterous union, he is cut off from the promises of the church, nor shall he who has deserted the church of Christ attain to the rewards of Christ; he is a stranger, an outsider, an enemy. He cannot have God as a father who has not the church as his mother. There was no escape for any who remained outside the ark of Noah; and even so he who is outside the Church cannot escape.

No Salvation Outside of the Church. (From Cyprian, *Epistle* LXII, 13 *ANF,* V, pp. 384-85.)

✓   ✓   ✓

Can the power of baptism be greater or of more avail than confession, than suffering, when one confesses Christ before men and is baptized in his own blood? And yet even this baptism does not benefit a heretic, although he has confessed Christ, and been put to death outside the Church, unless the patrons and advocates of heretics declare that the heretics who are slain in a false confession of Christ are martyrs, and assign to them the glory and the crown of martyrdom contrary to the testimony of the apostle, who says that it will profit them nothing although they were burnt and slain. But if not even the baptism of a public confession and blood can profit a heretic to salvation, because there is no salvation out of the Church, how much less shall it be of advantage to him, if in a hiding-place and a cave of robbers, stained with the contagion of adulterous water, he has not only put off his old sins, but rather heaped up still newer and greater ones!

— Reading No. 7 —

THE CHURCH AND SOCIETY

I. Against Warfare

From Tertullian, On The Crown *XI, ANF III, pp. 99-100.*

✦   ✦   ✦

To begin with the real ground of the military crown, I think we must first inquire whether warfare is proper at all for Christians. What sense is there in discussing the merely accidental, when that on which it rests is to be condemned? Do we believe it lawful for a human oath to be superadded to one divine, for a man to come under promise to another master after Christ, and to abjure father, mother, and all nearest kinsfolk, whom even the law has commanded us to honour and love next to God Himself, to whom the gospel, too, holding them only of less account than Christ, has in like manner rendered honor? Shall it be held lawful to make an occupation of the sword, when the Lord proclaims that he who uses the sword shall perish by the sword? And shall the son of peace take part in the battle when it does not become him even to sue at law? And shall he apply the chain, and the prison, and the torture, and the punishment, who is not the avenger even of his own wrongs? . . . shall he ask a watchword from the emperor who has already received one from God? Shall he be disturbed in death by the trumpet of the trumpeter, who expects to be aroused by the angel's trump? And shall the Christian be burned according to camp rule, when he was not permitted to burn incense to an idol, when to him Christ remitted the punishment of fire? Then how many other offences there are involved in the performances of camp

151

offices, which we must hold to involve a transgression of God's law, you may see by a slight survey. The very carrying of the name over from the camp of light to the camp of darkness is a violation of it. Of course, if faith comes later, and finds any preoccupied with military service, their case is different, as in the instance of those whom John used to receive for baptism, and of those most faithful centurions, I mean the centurion whom Christ approves, and the centurion whom Peter instructs; yet, at the same time, when a man has become a believer, and faith has been sealed, there must be either an immediate abandonment of it, which has been the course with many; or all sorts of quibbling will have to be resorted to in order to avoid offending God, and that is not allowed even outside of military service.

II. Forbidden Professions

From The Apostolic Tradition of Hippolytus, *pt. II, 16, translated by Burton S. Easton, op. cit., pp. 42-43.*

✓   ✓   ✓

Inquiry shall likewise be made about the professions and trades of those who are brought to be admitted to the faith. If a man is a pander, he must desist or be rejected. If a man is a sculptor or painter, he must be charged not to make idols; if he does not desist he must be rejected. If a man is an actor or pantomimist, he must desist or be rejected. A teacher of young children had best desist, but if he has no other occupation, he may be permitted to continue. A charioteer, likewise, who races or frequents races, must desist or be rejected. A gladiator or a trainer of gladiators, or a huntsman [in the wild beast shows] or anyone connected with these shows, or a public official in charge of gladiatorial exhibitions must desist or be rejected. A heathen priest or anyone who tends idols must desist or be rejected. A soldier of the civil authority must be taught not to kill men and refuse to do so if he is commanded, and to refuse to take an oath; if he is unwilling to comply, he must be rejected. A military commander or civic magistrate that wears the purple must resign or be rejected. If a catechumen or a believer seeks to become a soldier, they must be rejected, for they have despised God. A harlot or licentious man or one who has castrated himself, or any other who does things not to be named, must be rejected, for they are defiled. A magician must not [even] be brought for examination. An enchanter, an astrologer, a diviner, a soothsayer, a user of magic verses, a juggler, a mountebank, an amulet-maker must desist or be rejected. A concubine, who is a slave and has reared her children and has been faithful to her master alone, may become a hearer; but if she has failed in these matters she must be rejected. If a man has a concubine, he must desist and marry legally; if he is unwilling, he must be rejected.

III. In the World but not of the World.

From The Epistle to Diognetus V, *of the second or third century, translated by Kirsopp Lake,* The Apostolic Fathers, *Loeb Library.*

❧   ❧   ❧

For the distinction between Christians and other men is neither in country nor language nor customs. For they do not dwell in cities in some place of their own, nor do they use any strange variety of dialect, nor practise an extraordinary kind of life. This teaching of theirs has not been discovered by the intellect or thought of busy men, nor are they the advocates of any human doctrine as some men are. Yet while living in Greek and barbarian cities, according as each obtained his lot, and following the local customs, both in clothing and food and in the rest of life, they show forth the wonderful and confessedly strange character of the constitution of their own citizenship. They dwell in their own fatherlands, but as if sojourners in them; they share all things as citizens, and suffer all things as strangers. . . . To put it shortly, what the soul is in the body the Christians are in the world. . . . The flesh hates the soul, and wages war upon it, though it has suffered no evil, because it is prevented from gratifying its pleasures, and the world hates the Christians though it has suffered no evil, because they are opposed to its pleasures. The soul loves the flesh

which hates it and the limbs, and Christians love those
that hate them. The soul has been shut up in the body,
but itself sustains the body; and Christians are confined
in the world as in a prison, but themselves sustain the
world. The soul dwells immortal in a mortal tabernacle,
and Christians sojourn among corruptible things, waiting
for the incorruptibility which is in heaven. The soul when
evil treated in food and drink becomes better, and Christians, when buffeted, day by day increase more. God has
appointed them to so great a post and it is not right for
them to decline it.

IV. Poverty Pagan and Christian

A. Pagan Poverty. *The Ideal of the Cynic from Pseudo-Lucian,* Cynicus, *translated in A. C. Lovejoy and George Boas,* Primitivism and Related Ideas in Antiquity (*Baltimore: The Johns Hopkins Press, 1935*) *p. 143.*

✓   ✓   ✓

For all that costly array of means of enjoyment which
you so gloat over is obtained only at the price of labor
of the body and vexation of the mind. Consider, if you
please, the gold that is so sought after, the silver, the
luxurious houses, the elaborate clothing—and then remember through how much toil and trouble and danger
these have been acquired—yes, and through how many
men's blood and death and ruin. To bring these things
to you, many seamen must perish; to find and fashion
them, many laborers must endure misery. Nor is that all:
conflicts often arise because of them, and the desire for
them sets friend against friend, children against parents,
wives against husbands. . . . And all this goes on in spite
of the fact that embroidered clothes are no warmer than
others, houses with gilded roofs keep out the rain no
better; a drink out of a silver cup—or a gold one, for that
matter—is no more refreshing, and sleep is no sweeter
on an ivory bed—the reverse, in fact, is true; your 'happy'
man, between the delicate sheets on his ivory bed, is often
unable to sleep. As for all the trouble that is devoted to
the preparation of fancy dishes, it is needless to say that
it contributes nothing to our nourishment; on the contrary, such dishes injure the body and breed diseases in

it. No need, either, to mention all the things that men do and suffer for the sake of sexual gratification—though that desire is easy enough to satisfy, if one is not too fastidious about it. But it is not in this only that men show their madness and corruption; nowadays they pervert everything from its natural use—like a man who insists on treating a couch not as a couch but a carriage. . . .

Again, when people use edible things not for food but for making dyes—the murex, for example—are they not using the gifts of God in a way that is contrary to nature? . . . You can force a mixing bowl to do the work of a stew-pot; but that is not what it was made for.—However, it is impossible to mention all the ways that such people have of being mad; the number is too great. And you reproach me because I will not join in this madness; My life is like that of the well-behaved guest I described; I fare excellently on whatever is placed before me, I enjoy the things that it costs least trouble to prepare, and I have no craving for all those numerous and variegated dishes.

B. Christian Poverty

1. From Clement of Alexandria, The Instructor *II, iii, ANF II, 247 (slightly altered).*

For tell me, does the table-knife not cut unless it be studded with silver, and have its handle made of ivory? Or must we forgo Indian steel in order to divide meat, as when we call for a weapon for the fight? What if the basin be of earthenware? will it not receive the dirt of the hands? or the footpan the dirt of the foot? Will the table that is fashioned with ivory feet resent bearing a loaf that sells for an obol? Will the lamp not dispense light because it is the work of the potter, not of the goldsmith? I affirm that truckle-beds afford no worse repose than the ivory couch; and the goatskin coverlet being amply sufficient to spread on the bed, there is no need of purple or scarlet coverings. Yet to condemn, notwithstanding, frugality, through the stupidity of luxury, the author of mischief, what a prodigious error, what senseless conceit! See. The Lord ate from a common bowl, and made the disciples recline on the grass on the ground, and washed their feet, girded with a linen towel—He, the lowly-minded God, and Lord of the universe. He did not bring down a silver foot-bath from heaven. He asked to drink of the Samaritan woman, who drew the water from the well in an earthenware vessel, not seeking regal gold, but teaching us how to quench thirst easily. For He made use, not extravagance His aim. And He ate and drank at feasts, not digging metals from the earth, nor using vessels of gold and silver.

2. From Cyprian, Epistle 1, 12-14, ANF V, 279-80.

But those, moreover, whom you consider rich, who add forests to forests, and who, excluding the poor from their neighborhood, stretch out their fields far and wide into space without any limits, who possess immense heaps of silver and gold and mighty sums of money, either in built-up heaps or in buried stores,—even in the midst of their riches those are torn to pieces by the anxiety of vague thought, lest the robber should spoil, lest the murderer should attack, lest the envy of some wealthier neighbour should become hostile, and harass them with malicious lawsuits. Such a one enjoys no security either in his food or in his sleep. In the midst of the banquet he sighs, although he drinks from a jewelled goblet; and when his luxurious bed has enfolded his body, languid with feasting, in its yielding bosom, he lies wakeful in the midst of the down; nor does he perceive, poor wretch, that these things are merely gilded torments that he is held in bondage by his gold, and that he is the slave of his luxury and wealth rather than their master.

Hence, then, the one peaceful and trustworthy tranquillity, the one solid and firm and constant security, is this, for a man to withdraw from these eddies of a distracting world, and, anchored on the ground of the harbour of salvation, to lift his eyes from earth to heaven; . . .

Ceilings enriched with gold, and houses adorned with mosaics of costly marble, will seem mean to you, now when you know that it is you yourself who are rather to be perfected, you who are rather to be adorned, and that that dwelling in which God has dwelt as in a temple, in which the Holy Spirit has begun to make His abode, is of more importance than all others. Let is embellish this house with the colours of innocence, let us enlighten it with the light of justice: this will never fall into decay with the wear of age, nor shall it be defiled by the tarnishing of the colours of its walls, nor of its gold. Whatever is artificially beautified is perishing; and such things as contain not the reality of possession afford no abiding assurance to their possessors. But this remains in a beauty perpetually vivid, in perfect honour, in permanent splendour. It can neither decay nor be destroyed; . . .

3. From Tertullian, On the Apparel of Women V. ANF V, 16.

But if it is from the quality of utility that gold and silver derive their glory, why iron and brass excel them; . . . At all events, neither is the field tilled by means of gold, nor the ship fastened together by the strength of silver. No mattock plunges a golden edge into the ground; no nail drives a silver point into planks. I leave unnoticed the fact that the needs of our whole life are dependent upon iron and brass; whereas those rich materials themselves, requiring both to be dug up out of mines, and needing a forging process in every use (to which they are put), are helpless without the laborious vigour of iron and brass. Already, therefore, we must judge whence it is that so high dignity accrues to gold and silver, since they get precedence over material substances which are not only cousin-german to them in point of origin, but more powerful in point of usefulness.

4. The Discipline for Martyrdom from Tertullian, ibid., xiii, ANF V, 25.

For such delicacies as tend by their softness and effeminacy to unman the manliness of faith are to be discarded. Otherwise, I know not whether the wrist that has been wont to be surrounded with the palmleaf-like bracelet will endure till it grow into the numb hardness of its own chain. I know not whether the leg that has rejoiced in the anklet will suffer itself to be squeezed into the gyve! I fear the neck, beset with pearl and emerald nooses, will give no room to the broad-sword! Wherefore, blessed (sisters), let us meditate on hardships, and we shall not feel them; let us abandon luxuries, and we shall not regret them. Let us stand ready to endure every violence, having nothing which we may fear to leave behind. It is these things which are the bonds which retard our hope. Let us cast away earthly ornaments if we desire heavenly. Love not gold; . . . But Christians always and now more than ever, pass their times not in gold but in iron; the stoles of martyrdom are (now) preparing.

— Reading No. 8 —

CHRISTIANITY THE FAVORED
RELIGION OF THE EMPIRE

I. The Toleration Edict of Galerius, April 30, 311

From Lactantius, On the Deaths of the Persecutors, *xxxiv, translated in J. Stevenson,* op. cit., *p. 256.*

✓   ✓   ✓

Amongst our other arrangements, which we are making for the permanent advantage of the state, we had heretofore endeavoured to set all things right according to the ancient laws and public order of the Romans. It has been our special care that the Christians, too, who had left the persuasion of their forefathers should return to a better mind; since through some strange reasoning such wilfulness had seized the said Christians and such folly possessed them that, instead of following those constitutions of the ancients which peradventure their own ancestors had first established, they were making themselves laws for their own observance, merely according to their own judgment and as their pleasure was, and in diverse places were assembling various multitudes. In short, when our order had been set forth to the effect that they should betake themselves to the institutions of the ancients, many of them were subdued by danger, many also exposed to jeopardy. Nevertheless very great numbers held to their determination, and we saw that these neither gave worship and due reverence to the gods, nor yet worshipped the god of the Christians—we therefore in consideration of our most mild clemency, and of the unbroken custom whereby we are used to grant pardon to all men, have thought it right in this case also to offer our speediest indulgence, that Christians may exist again, and may establish their meeting houses, yet so that they do nothing contrary to good order. By another letter we shall signify to magistrates how they should proceed. Wherefore, in accordance with this our indulgence it will be their duty to pray their god for our estate, and that of the state, and their own, that the commonwealth may endure on every side unharmed, and they may be able to live securely in their habitations.

II. The Edict of Milan, A.D. 313

From Lactantius, op. cit., *XLVIII, 2-12, in Stevenson* op. cit., *260.*

✓   ✓   ✓

When we, Constantine Augustus and Licinius Augustus, had happily met at Milan, and were conferring about all things which concern the advantage and security of the state, we thought that amongst other things which seemed likely to profit men generally, the reverence paid to the Divinity merited our first and chief attention. Our purpose is to grant both to the Christians and to all others full authority to follow whatever worship each man has desired; whereby whatsoever Divinity dwells in heaven may be benevolent and propitious to us, and to all who are placed under our authority. Therefore we thought it salutary and most proper to establish our purpose that no man whatever should be refused complete toleration, who has given up his mind either to the cult of the Christians, or to the religion which he personally feels best suited to himself; to the end that the supreme Divinity, to whose worship we devote ourselves under no compulsion, may continue in all things to grant us his wanted favour and beneficence. Wherefore your Dignity should know that it is our pleasure to abolish all conditions whatever which were embodied in former orders directed to your office about the Christians, that what appeared utterly inauspicious and foreign to our Clemency should be done away and that every one of those who have a common wish to follow the religion of the Christians may from this moment freely and unconditionally proceed to observe the same without any annoyance or disquiet. These things we thought good to signify in the fullest manner to your Carefulness, that you might know that we have given freely and unreservedly to the said Christians toleration to practise their cult. And when you perceive that we have granted this favour to the said Christians, your Devotion understands that to others also freedom for their own worship and cult is likewise left open and freely granted, as befits the quiet of our times, that every man may have complete toleration in the practice of whatever worship he has chosen. This has been done by us that no diminution be made from the honour of any religion. Moreover in regard to the legal position of the Christians we have thought fit to ordain this also, that if any appear to have bought, whether from our exchequer or from any others, the places at which they were used formerly to assemble, concerning which definite orders have been given before now, and that by a letter issued to your office—that the same be restored to the Christians, setting aside all delay and doubtfulness, without any payment or demand of price. Those also who have obtained them by gift shall restore them in like manner without delay to the said Christians. And those moreover who have bought them, as well as those who have obtained them by gift, if they request anything of our benevolence, shall apply to the Vicarius, that order may be taken for them too by our Clemency. All these things must be delivered over at once and without delay by your intervention to the corporation of the Christians. And since the said Christians are known to have possessed, not those places only whereto they were used to assemble, but others also belonging to their corporation, namely to their churches, and not to individuals, we comprise them all under the above law, so that you will order them to be restored without any doubtfulness or dispute to the said Christians, that is to their corporation and assemblies; provided always as aforesaid, that those who restore them without price, as we said, shall expect a compensation from our benevolence. In all these things you must give the aforesaid Christians your most effective intervention, that our command may be fulfilled as soon as may be, and that in this matter, as well as others, order may be

taken by our Clemency for the public quiet. So far we
will ensure that, as has been already stated, the Divine
favour toward us which we have already experienced in
so many affairs shall continue for all time to give us
prosperity and successes, together with happiness for the
State. But that the tenor of our gracious ordinance may
be brought to the knowledge of all men, it will be your
duty by a proclamation of your own to publish everywhere and bring to the notice of all men this present
document, that the command of this our benevolence may
not be hidden.

III. The Political Theory of the Christian Roman Empire

From Eusebius, Oration on Constantine *XVI, PNF Ser. 2,
vol. 1, pp. 606-07. Translation revised.*

✦   ✦   ✦

Of old the nations of the earth, the entire human race,
were variously distributed into provincial, national, and
local governments, subject to kingdoms and principalities
of many kinds. The consequences of this variety were
war and strife, depopulation and captivity. . . . The
origin of these may justly be ascribed to the delusion of
polytheistic error. But when that instrument of our redemption, the thrice holy body of Christ was raised . . .
the energy of these evil spirits was at once destroyed. The
manifold forms of government, the tyrannies and repub-
lics, the siege of cities, and devastation of countries caused
thereby, were now no more, and one God was proclaimed
to all mankind. At the same time one universal power,
the Roman empire, arose and flourished, while the enduring and implacable hatred of nation against nation was
not removed. . . . Our Savior's mighty power destroyed
at once the many governments and the many gods of the
demons and proclaimed to all men, both Greek and barbarian, to the extremities of the earth, the sole sovereignty
of God himself. Meantime the Roman empire, the causes
of multiplied governments being thus removed, effected
an easy conquest of those which yet remained; its object
being to unite all nations in one symphonic whole; an
object in great measure already secured, and destined to

be still more perfectly attained, even to the final conquest of the ends of the habitable world. . . . The falsehood of demon superstition was convicted: the inveterate strife and mutual hatred of the nations was removed: at the same time One God, and the knowledge of that God, were proclaimed to all: one universal empire prevailed; and the whole human race, subdued by the controlling power of peace and concord, received one another as brethren, and responded to the feelings of their kindred nature. Hence, as children of one God and Father, and owning true religion as their common mother, they saluted and welcomed each other with words of peace. Thus the whole world appeared like one well-ordered and united family: each one might journey unhindered as far as and whithersoever he pleased: men might securely travel from West to East, and from East to West, as to their own native country: in short the ancient oracle and predictions of the prophets were fulfilled, "And they shall beat their swords into plough-shares, and their spears into sickles: and nation shall not take up sword against nation, neither shall they learn war any more."

THE EMPIRE AND THE CHURCH

I. Controversy in the West: The Donatist Affair

The canons of the Council of Arles in A.D. 314, relating to the Donatists. Information and translation in Stevenson, op. cit., p. 322-24.

✐   ✐   ✐

Moreover, with regard to the Africans, forasmuch as they use their own law of re-baptizing, we have decreed that, if any heretic comes to the Church, he should be questioned concerning the Creed; and, if it be found that he has been baptized in the Father and the Son and the Holy Ghost, hands shall be laid upon him, and no more. But if, on being questioned as to the Creed, he does not give the Trinity in answer, then let him rightly be baptized. . . .

Concerning those who are said to have surrendered the Holy Scriptures or communion vessels, or the names of their brethren, we decree that whoever of them has been proved from public documents to have done these things shall be removed from the clergy. For if the same persons are found to have carried out ordinations, and a question has arisen about those whom they have ordained, such ordination should not be prejudicial to them. And seeing that there are many who seem to oppose the church, and through bribed witnesses think that they should be allowed to bring accusations, their plea is absolutely disallowed, unless, as we said above, they produce evidence from written documents. . . .

Concerning those who falsely accuse their brethren, we decree that they are not to communicate to the day of their death. . . .

Concerning those who apostasize and never claim readmission, and do not even seek to show repentance, and afterwards when they are ill, ask for communion, we decree that communion be not given to them, unless they recover and produce fruits worthy of repentance.

II. Controversy in the East: The Arian Affair

The Teaching of the Arians according to Socrates, Ecclesiastical History *1, v,* PNF *Ser. 2, vol. II, p. 4.*

The dogmas they have invented and assert, contrary to the Scriptures, are these: That God was not always the Father, but that there was a period when he was not the Father; that the Word of God was not from eternity, but was made out of nothing; . . . wherefore there was a time when he did not exist, inasmuch as the Son is a creature and a work. That he is neither like the Father as it regards his essence, nor is by nature either the Father's true Word, or true Wisdom, but indeed one of his works and creatures, being erroneously called Word and Wisdom, since he was himself made by God's own Word and the Wisdom which is in God, whereby God both made all things and him also. Wherefore he is as to his nature mutable and susceptible of change, as all other rational creatures are: hence the Word is alien to and other than the essence of God; and the Father is inexplicable by the Son, and invisible to him, for neither does the Word perfectly and accurately know the Father, neither can he distinctly see him. The Son knows not the nature of his own essence: for he was made on our account, in order that God might create us by him, as by an instrument; nor would he ever have existed, unless God had wished to create us.

Some one accordingly asked them whether the Word of God could be changed, as the devil has been? and they feared not to say, 'Yes, he could; for being begotten, he is susceptible of change.'

III. The Orthodox Creeds

A. The Creed of Nicaea. *The form now received and given below is that adopted at Constantinople at the*

Second Ecumenical Council in A.D. *381. It differed from the creed adopted at the Council of Nicaea in 325 by the omission of the anathemas and the phrase applied to Christ "of the substance of the Father." Some have supposed this excision to have been a concession to the Arians but this can scarcely have been so because the word* homoousios *was retained. Words in brackets were added in the Latin form in the West. The expression "and the Son" (filioque) became a source of great controversy between the Roman and the Greek churches. The Western Church holds that the Spirit proceeds from the Father and from the Son, but the Greek Church that the Spirit may come through wider channels. The text and translation are in Philip Schaff,* op. cit., *pp. 58-59.*

     ✓   ✓   ✓

I believe in one God the Father Almighty: Maker of heaven and earth, and of all things visible and invisible. And in one Lord Jesus Christ, the only-begotten Son of God, begotten of the Father before all worlds [*God of God*] Light of Light, very God of very God, begotten, not made, being of one substance [*essence*] with the Father; by whom all things were made; who, for us men and for our salvation, came down from heaven, and was incarnate by the Holy Ghost of the Virgin Mary, and was made man; and was crucified also for us under Pontius Pilate; he suffered and was buried; and ascended into heaven, and sitteth on the right hand of the Father; and he shall come again, with glory, to judge both the quick and the dead; whose kingdom shall have no end.

And in the Holy Ghost, the Lord and Giver of Life; who proceedeth from the Father [*and the Son*]; who with the Father and the Son together is worshipped and glorified: who spake by the prophets. And one Holy Catholic and Apostolic Church. I acknowledge one baptism for the remission of sins; and I look for the resurrection of the dead, and the life of the world to come. Amen.

The creed as adopted in A.D. *325 had the following anathemas against the Arians:*

But the holy Catholic and Apostolic Church anathematizes those who say, "There was a time when he was not," and "He was not before he was begotten," and "He was made from that which did not exist," and those who assert that he is of other substance or essence than the Father, or that he was created, or is susceptible of change.

B. The Creed of Chalcedon, A.D. 450. *The translation is from J. C. Ayer, A Source Book for Ancient Church History (New York: Charles Scribner's Sons, 1920), p. 520. Note the expression in two natures. The possible inference from in rather than of, that the union had been only temporary is precluded by the many adjectives.*

✓   ✓   ✓

Following the holy Fathers, we all with one voice teach men to confess that the Son and our Lord Jesus Christ is one and the same, that He is perfect in godhead and perfect in manhood, truly God and truly man, of a reasonable soul and body, consubstantial with His Father as touching His godhead, and consubstantial with us as to His manhood, in all things like unto us, without sin: begotten of His Father before all worlds according to His godhead; but in these last days for us and for our salvation of the Virgin Mary, the Theotokos, according to His manhood, one and the same Christ, Son, Lord, only begotten Son, in two natures, unconfusedly, immutably, indivisibly, inseparably; the distinction of natures being preserved and concurring in one person and hypostasis, not separated or divided into two persons, but one and the same Son and Only begotten, God the Word, the Lord Jesus Christ, as the prophets from the beginning have spoken concerning Him, and as the Lord Jesus Christ himself has taught us, and as the creed of the Fathers has delivered us.

REACTIONS AGAINST THE IMPERIAL CHURCH

I. The Bishops

The Protest of Hosius to the Emperor Constantius; Information and translation in Shotwell and Loomis, op. cit., *p. 578.*

✓ ✓ ✓

But if they [*the Arians*] pretend there was coercion and appreciate that it was wrong and if you too disapprove of it, then do you yourself refrain from coercion and write no letters and send no counts, but release those whom you have banished, lest, while you blame us for coercion, they use coercion still more violent upon us.

What wrong like this was ever done by Constans? What bishop was sent into exile? When did he act as arbiter of an ecclesiastical tribunal? Which of his palatines forced men to subscribe against anyone, as Valens and his fellows declare? Cease, I entreat you, and remember that you are a mortal. Fear the day of judgment and keep yourself pure against it. Intrude not yourself into the business of the Church and give no commandment to us regarding it but learn it instead from us. God has placed in your hands the Empire: to us he has committed the administration of his Church. And as he who would steal the government from you opposes the ordinance of God, even so do you fear lest by taking upon yourself the conduct of the Church, you make yourself guilty of a grave sin. It is written: "Render unto Caesar the things that are Caesar's and unto God the things that are God's." Therefore it is not permitted to us to bear rule on earth nor have you the right to burn incense. I write this out of anxiety for your salvation.

As for the purport of your letters, this is my resolution. I assuredly will not ally myself with the Arians and I anathematize their heresy. Nor will I subscribe to the condemnation of Athanasius, . . .

II. The Pagan Critique. Julian the Apostate

The works of Julian are translated in three volumes in the Loeb Library by W. C. Wright. The following passages are in volume III: A. Ep. 37, p. 123; B. Against the Galileans III, 327 A. p. 413; C. Ep. 47, pp. 145-47.

✓ ✓ ✓

A. On Toleration. . . . By the gods, I would neither have the Galileans put to death, nor scourged unjustly, nor in any other manner ill-treated. I think it, nevertheless, highly proper that the worshippers of the gods should be preferred to them. By the madness of the Galileans, the Empire was almost ruined, but by the goodness of the gods we are now preserved. We ought, therefore, to honour the gods, and also religious men and states.

And, for the future, let the people agree among themselves; let no one be at variance, or do an injury to another; neither you, who are in error, to those who worship the gods, rightly and justly, in the mode transmitted to us from the most ancient times; nor let the worshippers of the gods destroy or plunder the houses of those who rather by ignorance than choice are led astray. Men should be taught and persuaded by reason, not by blows, invectives and corporal punishments. I therefore again and again admonish those who embrace the true religion in no respect to injure or insult the Galileans, neither by attacks nor reproaches. We should rather pity than hate those who in the most important concerns act ill.

B. Christianity Corrupted. But you are so misguided that you have not even remained faithful to the teachings that were handed down to you by the apostles. And these also have been altered, so as to be worse and more impious, by those who came after. At any rate neither Paul

nor Matthew nor Luke nor Mark ventured to call Jesus
God. But the worthy John, since he perceived that a
great number of people in many of the towns of Greece
and Italy had already been infected by this disease, and
because he heard, I suppose, that even the tombs of
Peter and Paul were being worshipped—secretly, it is
true, but still he did hear this,—he, I say, was the first to
venture to call Jesus God.

C. Christianity not suitable to Empire. I am overwhelmed
with shame, I affirm it by the gods, O men of Alexandria,
to think that even a single Alexandrian can admit that he
is a Galilean. The forefathers of the genuine Hebrews
were the slaves of the Egyptians long ago, but in these
days, men of Alexandria, you who conquered the Egyptians—for your founder was the conqueror of Egypt—
submit yourselves, despite your sacred traditions, in willing slavery to men who have set at naught the teachings
of their ancestors. You have then no recollection of those
happy days of old when all Egypt held communion with
the gods and we enjoyed many benefits therefrom. But
those who have but yesterday introduced among you
this new doctrine, tell me of what benefit have they been
to the city? Your founder was a god-fearing man, Alexander of Macedon, in no way, by Zeus, like any of these
persons, nor again did he resemble any Hebrews, though
the latter have shown themselves far superior to the
Galileans.

III. Monasticism

Of Mortification *from Cassian of Marseilles translated
by Helen Waddell,* The Desert Fathers (*Ann Arbor: Ann
Arbor Books, University of Michigan Press, 1957. Quoted
by permission of Constable and Company Limited, London*), *pp. 160-62.*

The abbot Abraham . . . was silent for a long while,
and then with a heavy sigh, at last he spoke. . . .
We could have built our cells in the valley of the
Nile, and had water at our door, nor been driven to
bring it to our mouths from three miles off. . . . We

are not ignorant that in our land there are fair and
secret places, where there be fruit trees in plenty and the
graciousness of gardens, and the richness of the land
would give us our daily bread with very little bodily toil.
. . . But we have despised àll these and with them all the
luxurious pleasure of the world: we have joy in this
desolation, and to all delight do we prefer the dread
vastness of this solitude, nor do we weigh the riches of
your glebe against these bitter sands. . . . It is a little
thing that a monk should have made a single renunciation, that is, in the first days of his calling to have
trampled on things present, unless he persist in renounc-
ing them daily. Up to the very end of this life the word
of the Prophet must be in our mouths: 'And the day of
man Thou knowest I have not desired.' Whence the saying of the Lord in the Gospel, 'If any man will come
after me, let him deny himself, and take up his cross
daily, and follow me.'

And so he who keeps an anxious watch over the purity
of the inner man will seek those places which have no
rich fertility to seduce his mind to their tilling, nor be-
guile him from his fixed and motionless abiding in his
cell to work that is to be done under the sky, whereby
his thoughts are emptied out in the open, and all direction of the mind and that keen vision of its goal are scattered over diverse things: and this can be avoided by no
man, however anxious and vigilant, save he that shuts in
soul and body together within the fence of his walls.
Like a mighty fisherman, in the apostle's fashion, per-
ceiving his food in the depths of his most quiet heart,
intent and motionless he catches the swimming shoal of
his thoughts: and gazing curiously into the depths as from
an upstanding rock, judges what fish a man may whole-
somely draw in, and which he may pass by or throw out,
as bad and poisonous. . . .

What difficulty and labour there be in this, the experience of those that dwell in the desert of Calamus or
Porphyrio doth manifestly prove. For they are divided
from all towns and habitations of men by a vaster stretch
of desert than even Scete is (for hardly in seven or eight
days may those who penetrate the wastes of that vast
solitude come at the secret of their cells), nevertheless

because they be tillers of the ground and confined in no cloister, when they come to the desolation amid which we live, or to that of Scete, they are harried by such tempests of imagination, by such perturbation of spirit, that they seem to be raw and unskilled in the lightest practises of solitude, and cannot endure the long tarrying in their cell and the stillness of the silence. For they have not learned to quiet the stirrings of the inner man and to beat up against the tempest of their thoughts with perpetual watchfulness and persevering intentness, these that sweat daily at work under the open heavens, all day under the windy emptiness, flitting hither and thither not only in body but in mind, and their thoughts scattering with the movement of their bodies over the open fields. They feel the many-winged folly of their soul, nor can they control its wanton forays: contrition of spirit comes hard to them, they find the perpetual silence intolerable, and these that no labour on the land could weary are vanquished by idleness and worn out by the long lasting of their peace.

IV. The Return: Monasticism Allied with Scholarship

Jerome's Preface to the Vulgate, A.D. *383, translated in Ayer*, op. cit., *p. 485.*

      ✔   ✔   ✔

You urge me to make a new work out of an old and, as it were, to sit in judgment on the copies of the Scriptures already scattered throughout the whole world; and, inasmuch as they differ among themselves, I am to decide which of them agree with the Greek original. A pious labor, but a perilous presumption; to judge others, myself to be judged of all; to change the language of the aged, and to carry back the world already grown gray, back to the beginnings of its infancy! Is there a man, learned or unlearned, who will not, when he takes the volume into his hands and perceives that what he reads differs from the flavor which once he tasted, break out immediately into violent language and call me a forger and a profane person for having the audacity to add anything to the ancient books or to change or correct anything? I am consoled in two ways in bearing this odium: in the first place, that you, the supreme bishop, command it to be done; and secondly, even on the testimony of those reviling us, what varies cannot be true. For if we put faith in the Latin texts, let them tell us which; for there are almost as many texts as copies. But if the truth is to be sought from many, why should we not go back to the original Greek and correct the mistakes introduced by inaccurate translators, and the blundering alterations of confident and ignorant men, and further, all that has been added or altered by sleepy copyists? I am not discussing the Old Testament, which was turned into Greek by the Seventy Elders, and has reached us by a descent of three steps. I do not ask what Aquila and Symmachus think, or why Theodotion takes a middle course between the ancients and the moderns. I am willing to let that be a true translation which had apostolic approval. I am now speaking of the New Testament. This was undoubtedly composed in Greek, with the exception of the work of the Apostle Matthew, who first published the gospel of Christ in Judea and in Hebrew. This, as it is in our language, is certainly marked by discrepancies, and the stream flows in different channels; it must be sought in one fountainhead. I pass over those manuscripts bearing the names of Lucian and Hesychius, which a few contentious persons perversely support. It was not permitted these writers to amend anything in the Old Testament after the labor of the Seventy; and it was useless to make corrections in the New, for translations of the Scriptures already made in the language of many nations show that they are additions and false. Therefore this short preface promises only the four gospels, of which the order is Matthew, Mark, Luke, and John, revised by a comparison of the Greek manuscripts and only of the ancient manuscripts. And that they might not depart far from the Latin customarily read, I have used my pen with some restraint, so that having corrected only the passages which seemed to change the meaning, I have allowed the rest to remain as it was.

THE CITY OF GOD
AND THE BYZANTINE CHURCH

I. The Earthly and the Heavenly Cities

Augustine's The City of God *XIX, 17* PNF *Ser. 1, vol. ii, pp. 412-13.*

✔   ✔   ✔

But the families which do not live by faith seek their peace in the earthly advantages of this life; while the families which live by faith look for those eternal blessings which are promised, and use as pilgrims such advantages of time and of earth as do not fascinate and divert them from God, but rather aid them to endure with greater ease, and to keep down the number of those burdens of the corruptible body which weigh upon the soul. . . . The heavenly city, or rather the part of it which sojourns on earth and lives by faith, makes use of this peace only because it must, until this mortal condition which necessitates it shall pass away. Consequently, so long as it lives like a captive and a stranger in the earthly city, though it has already received the promise of redemption, and the gift of the Spirit as the earnest of it, it makes no scruple to obey the laws of the earthly city, whereby the things necessary for the maintenance of this mortal life are administered; and thus, as this life is common to both cities, so there is a harmony between them in regard to what belongs to it. This heavenly city, then, while it sojourns on earth, calls citizens out of all nations, and gathers together a society of pilgrims of all languages, not scrupling about diversities in the manners, laws, and institutions whereby earthly peace is secured and maintained, but recognizing that, however various these are, they all tend to one and the same end of earthly peace. It therefore is so far from rescinding and abolishing these diversities, that it even preserves and adopts them, so long only as no hindrance to the worship of the one supreme and true God is thus introduced. Even the heavenly city, therefore, while in its state of pilgrimage, avails itself of the peace of earth, and, so far as it can without injuring faith and godliness, desires and maintains a common agreement among men regarding the acquisition of the necessaries of life, and makes this earthly peace bear upon the peace of heaven; for this alone can be truly called and esteemed the peace of the reasonable creatures, consisting as it does in the perfectly ordered and harmonious enjoyment of God and of one another in God. When we shall have reached that peace, this mortal life shall give place to one that is eternal, and our body shall be no more this animal body which by its corruption weighs down the soul, but a spiritual body feeling no want, and in all its members subjected to the will. In its pilgrim state the heavenly city possesses this peace by faith; and by this faith it lives righteously when it refers to the attainment of that peace every good action towards God and man; for the life of the city is a social life.

The Church Fulfills the Predictions of the Messianic Age, ibid., *XX, 9, p. 430.*

✓   ✓   ✓

It is then of this kingdom militant, in which conflict with the enemy is still maintained, and war carried on with warring lusts, or government laid upon them as they yield, until we come to that most peaceful kingdom in which we shall reign without an enemy, and it is of this first resurrection in the present life, that the Apocalypse speaks in the words just quoted. For, after saying that the devil is bound a thousand years and is afterwards loosed for a short season, it goes on to give a sketch of what the Church does or of what is done in the Church in those days, in the words, "And I saw seats and them that sat upon them, and judgment was given." It is not to be supposed that this refers to the last judgment, but to the seats of the rulers and to the rulers themselves by whom the Church is now governed. And no better interpretation of judgment being given can be produced than that which we have in the words, "What ye bind on earth shall be bound in heaven; and what ye loose on earth shall be loosed in heaven." . . . The Church, then, begins its reign with Christ now in the living and in the dead.

But true Felicity is reserved for Heaven, ibid., *XXX, 30, pp. 509-10.*

✓   ✓   ✓

How great shall be that felicity, which shall be tainted with no evil, which shall lack no good, and which shall afford leisure for the praises of God, who shall be all in all! For I know not what other employment there can be where no lassitude shall slacken activity, nor any want stimulate to labor. I am admonished also by the sacred song, in which I read or hear the words, "Blessed are they that dwell in Thy house, O Lord; they will be still praising Thee."
   . . . One thing is certain, the body shall forthwith be wherever the spirit wills, and the spirit shall will nothing which is unbecoming either to the spirit or to the body. True honor shall be there, for it shall be denied to none who is worthy, nor yielded to any unworthy; neither shall any unworthy person so much as sue for it, for none but the worthy shall be there. True peace shall be there, where no one shall suffer opposition either from himself or any other. God Himself, who is the Author of virtue, shall there be its reward; for, as there is nothing greater or better, He has promised Himself. What else was meant by His word through the prophet, "I will be your God, and ye shall be my people," than, I shall be their satisfaction, I shall be all that men honorably desire,—life, and health, and nourishment, and plenty, and glory, and honor, and peace, and all good things? This, too, is the right interpretation of the saying of the apostle, "That God may be all in all."

II. Justinian's Laws Against Pagans

Codex *I, II from Ayer,* op. cit., *pp. 558-60.*

Because some are found who are imbued with the error of the impious and detestable pagans, and do those things which move a merciful God to just wrath, and that we may not suffer ourselves to leave uncorrected matters which concern these things, but, knowing that they have abandoned the worship of the true and only God, and have in insane error offered sacrifices, and, filled with all impiety, have celebrated solemnities, we subject those who have committed these things, after they have been held worthy of holy baptism, to the punishment appropriate to the crimes of which they have been convicted; but for the future we decree to all by this present law that they who have been made Christians and at any time have been deemed worthy of the holy and saving baptism, if it appear that they have remained still in the error of the pagans, shall suffer capital punishment.

(1) Those who have not yet been worthy of the venerable rite of baptism shall report themselves, if they dwell in this royal city or in the provinces, and go to the holy churches with their wives and children and all the household subject to them, and be taught the true faith of Christians, so that having been taught their former error henceforth to be rejected, they may receive saving baptism, or know, if they regard these things of small value, that they are to have no part in all those things which belong to our commonwealth, neither is it permitted them to become owners of anything movable or immovable, but, deprived of everything, they are to be left in poverty, and besides are subject to appropriate penalties.

(2) We forbid also that any branch of learning be taught by those who labor under the insanity of the impious pagans, so that they may not for this reason pretend that they instruct those who unfortunately resort to them, but in reality corrupt the minds of their pupils; and let them not receive any support from the public treasury, since they are not permitted by the Holy Scriptures or by

pragmatic forms [public decrees] to claim anything of the sort for themselves. . . .

(3) For if any one here or in the provinces shall have been convicted of not having hastened to the holy churches with his wife and children, as said, he shall suffer the aforesaid penalties, and the fisc shall claim his property, and they shall be sent into exile.

(4) If any one in our commonwealth, hiding himself, shall be discovered to have celebrated sacrifices or the worship of idols, let him suffer the same capital punishment as the Manichaeans. . . .

BIBLIOGRAPHY

General Histories of the Christian Church:

Walker, Williston, *A History of the Christian Church* (revised 1959).

Latourette, Kenneth Scott, *A History of Christianity* (1953).

Histories of the Early Church:

Lietzmann, Hans, *The Beginnings of the Christian Church*, 4 vols. (1937-8).

Kidd, B. J., *A History of the Church to A.D. 461*, 3 vols. (1922).

Duchesne, Louis, *Early History of the Christian Church*, 3 vols. (1909-24).

Hodges, George, *The Early Church* (1915).

Carrington, Philip, *The Early Christian Church*, 2 vols. (1927).

Sources:

Most of the early Christian literature is available in the Ante-Nicene Fathers *and the* Post-Nicene Fathers, *series one and series two. New translations are in progress:* The Fathers of the Church (*Catholic*) *and* The Library of Christian Classics (*Protestant*). *Collections of excerpts are available in:*

Ayer, J. C., *A Source Book for Ancient Church History* (1920).

Kidd, B. J., *Documents Illustrative of the Early Church*, 3 vols. (1920).

Gwatkin, H. M., *Selections from Early Writers Illustrative of Church History to the Time of Constantine* (1893).

Stevenson, J., *A New Eusebius* (1957).

Grant, Frederick C., *Hellenistic Religions* (1953), pagan background.

Grant, Robert M., *Second-Century Christianity* (1946).

Owen, E. C. E., *Some Authentic Acts of the Early Martyrs* (1927).

Shotwell, J. T., and Loomis, Louise R., *The See of Peter* (1927).
Wright, F. A., *Fathers of the Church* (1929), Latin Fathers only.

The Persecutions:

Hardy, E. G., *Christianity and the Roman Government* (1925).
Workman, H. B., *Persecution in the Early Church* (1906).
Goodenough, Erwin, *The Church in the Roman Empire* (1931).
Stauffer, Ethelbert, *Christ and the Caesars* (1948).

Rival Religious Systems:

Angus, Samuel, *The Religious Quests of the Graeco-Roman World* (1929).
———, *The Mystery Religions and Christianity* (1928).
Cumont, Franz, *The Oriental Religions in Roman Paganism* (1911).
———, *The Mysteries of Mithra* (1903).
Frazer, James G., *Attis, Adonis and Osiris* (1906).
———, *The Golden Bough* (abridged in one volume, 1923).
Nock, A. D., *Conversion* (1933).
Willoughby, H. R., *Pagan Regeneration* (1929).
Cochrane, C. N., *Christianity and Classical Culture* (1940).
Carrington, Philip, *Christian Apologetics* (1921).
Jonas, Hans, *The Gnostic Religion* (1958).
Mead, G. R. S., *Pistis Sophia* (1896), translation of a Gnostic work.

Internal Development of the Church:

Harnack, Adolf, *Mission and Expansion*, 3 vols. (1908).
Latourette, Kenneth Scott, *History of the Expansion of Christianity*, vol. 1 (1937).
Hatch, Edwin, *The Organization of the Early Christian Churches* (1881).
Lowrie, W., *The Church and its Organization* (1904).
Marucchi, O., *Manual of Christian Archeology* (1935).
Duchesne, Louis, *Christian Worship* (1931).
Watkins, O. D., *History of Penance*, 2 vols. (1920).
Souter, A., *The Text and Canon of the New Testament* (1913).
James, M. R., *The Apocryphal New Testament* (1924).
Bethune-Baker, J. F., *An Introduction to the Early History of Christian Doctrine* (1903, reprint 1958).

Kelly, J. N. D., *Early Christian Creeds* (1950).
———, *Early Christian Doctrines* (1958).
Cadoux, C. J., *The Early Church and the World* (1925).
Giordani, Igino, *The Social Message of the Early Church Fathers* (1944).

The Christian Roman Empire:

Baker, G. P., *Constantine the Great* (1930).
Baynes, Norman H., *Constantine the Great and the Christian Church* (1930).
Alfoeldi, András, *The Conversion of Constantine and Pagan Rome* (1948).
Doerries, Hermann, *Constantine and Religious Liberty* (1960).
Frend, W. H. C., *The Donatist Church* (1952).
Gwatkin, H. M., *The Arian Controversy* (1889).
Simpson, W. D., *Julian the Apostate* (1930).
Workman, H. B., *The Evolution of the Monastic Ideal* (1913).
Adeney, W. F., *The Greek and Eastern Churches* (1908).
Kidd, B. J., *The Churches of Eastern Christendom* (1927).

Biography:

Farrar, F. W., *Lives of the Fathers,* 2 vols. (1889).
Campenhausen, Hans, *The Fathers of the Greek Church* (1959).
Richardson, Cyril, *The Christianity of Ignatius* (1935).
Goodenough, Erwin, *The Theology of Justin Martyr* (1923).
Hitchcock, F. R. M., *Irenaeus* (1914).
Morgan, J., *Importance of Tertullian* (1928).
Benson, E. W., *Cyprian* (1897).
Tollinton, R. B., *Clement of Alexandria* (1914).
Daniélou, Jean, *Origen* (1955).
Monceaux, F., *St. Jerome* (1933).
Prestige, G. L., *St. Basil the Great* (1956).
Attwater, D., *St. John Chrysostom* (1939).
Dudden, F. H., *Life and Times of St. Ambrose,* 2 vols. (1935).
Battenhouse, Roy, *A Companion to the Study of St. Augustine* (1955), symposium.
Bourke, Vernon J., *Augustine's Quest of Wisdom* (1945).
D'Arcy, M. C., *A Monument to St. Augustine* (1930), symposium.
Figgis, J. N., *The Political Aspect of St. Augustine's City of God* (1921).

CHRONOLOGICAL TABLE OF EMPERORS, CHURCH FATHERS, AND EVENTS

Philo* after 40
Caligula emp. 37-41
Nero persecution 64
Paul and Peter*
Domitian persecution 95
Clement of Rome 95
Pliny to Trajan c.112
Ignatius* c.110-117
Tacitus* after 117
Marcion's schism 144
Hermas c.140
Polycarp* 156
Justin Martyr* c.165
Vienne & Lyons persecution 177
Irenaeus bishop 178
Victor Roman bishop 189-98
Quartodecimanism c.190
Valentinus c.160-70
Celsus c.180
Canon of New Testament c.200
Septimius Severus persecution 202
Tertullian c.155-c.222
Callistus Roman bishop 217-222
Elgabal emp. 218-222
Hippolytus* 235
Alexander Severus emp. 222-235
Cyprian bishop 248
Origen* 254
Decius persecution 250
Novatian c.250
Plotinus 244-70
Gallienus toleration 261

Paul of Samosata tried 268
Mani* 276
Diocletian persecution 302-4
Galerius toleration 311
Donatism 311 f.
Constantine wins Rome 312
Milan edict 313
Lactantius c.260-c.340
Arles Synod 314
Constantine sole emp. 324
Nicaea Council 325
Eusebius of Caesarea c.260-340
Arius excommunicated 320
Athanasius bishop 328
Liberius Roman bishop 352-66
Hosius c.257-359
Constantine II * 340
Constans* 350
Constantius sole emp. 350-61
Julian emp. 361-63
Ambrose bishop 373
Jerome c.340-420
Chrysostom c.345-407
Theodosius I emp. 379-95
Augustine: conversion 386 bishop 395* 430
Ephesus Council 431
Theodosian code 438
"Robber" Council 449
Chalcedon Council 450
Justinian emp. 527-65

* Died.

INDEX